TRAVELL

CAMBODIA

By
ANDREW FORBES & DAVID HENLEY

Written by Andrew Forbes and David Henley

Published by Thomas Cook Publishing
A division of Thomas Cook Tour Operations Limited.
Company registration no. 1450464 England
The Thomas Cook Business Park, Unit 9, Coningsby Road,
Peterborough PE3 8SB, United Kingdom
E-mail: books@thomascook.com, Tel: + 44 (0) 1733 416477
www.thomascookpublishing.com

Produced by Cambridge Publishing Management Limited
Burr Elm Court, Main Street, Caldecote CB23 7NU

ISBN: 978-1-84157-989-4

© 2008 Thomas Cook Publishing
Text © Thomas Cook Publishing
Maps © Thomas Cook Publishing/PCGraphics (UK) Limited

Series Editor: Maisie Fitzpatrick
Production/DTP: Steven Collins

Printed and bound in Italy by Printer Trento

Cover photography: Front L–R: © Gavin Hellier/Photographer's Choice/Getty;
© Pavan Aldo/4Corners Images; © Joson/Corbis
Back L–R: © Hugh Sitton/Corbis; © Jim Holmes/Axiom Photographic
Agency/Getty

Contents

4

Introduction

For most of the second half of the 20th century, Cambodia was racked by war and famine. Considered a 'sideshow' in the Second Indochina War (better known as the Vietnam War), it was invaded by both North and South Vietnam, bombed to bits by the United States, strewn with land mines and lethal weapons of every kind, and – worst of all – ruled, between 1975 and 1979, by the genocidal Khmer Rouge regime headed by Pol Pot.

Things were so bad that the very name 'Cambodia' became synonymous with suffering. Yet it was not always like this. Before becoming a battlefield in the mid-1960s, the country was celebrated as a land of fertile tranquillity where a predominantly Buddhist people continued the artistic and cultural traditions of the old Khmer Empire – the first high civilisation in Southeast Asia, still exemplified by the extraordinary temples of Angkor Wat, surely the Eighth Wonder of the World.

For most of the last two decades Cambodia, now once again at peace, has striven to rebuild both its economy and its image. Central to this endeavour is tourism, which the Phnom Penh government is sparing no effort in promoting. At the heart of this programme is the temple complex at Angkor, which has been cleared of land mines and is currently undergoing extensive restoration. Angkor has to be seen to be believed. It is, beyond doubt, the major cultural and historic attraction in all of Southeast Asia, and it is difficult to think of any site of comparable magnificence anywhere else in the world.

Still, there is more to Cambodia than Angkor. Other ancient temple complexes are becoming increasingly accessible to visitors, including Preah Vihear, isolated on a remote cliff top by the Thai frontier and still only easily visited from northeast Thailand. In addition to temples, Phnom Penh – a once elegant city of broad boulevards and riverside cafés set by the *chatomuk*, or confluence of the Mekong, Sap and Bassac Rivers – is fast regaining its old appeal, and is home to the spectacular Royal Palace and the excellent National Museum.

Then there is the southern coast, where the seaside resorts of Kompong Som and Kep – the latter razed to the ground by the vengeful Khmer Rouge – provide great swimming, diving and other water sports. Two former hill stations, Bokor and Kirirom, are currently being restored as quiet and cool rural retreats from the heat of the plains, and in the east of the country the mighty Mekong River offers wonderful opportunities for river cruising, fishing and even freshwater dolphin watching.

In the centre of the country the huge lake called Tonlé Sap also merits mention. The very heart of Cambodia's rich agricultural and fishing economies, it is the fresh water source on which much of the country's prosperity depends. During the annual monsoon rains it increases several times in size, becoming a natural reservoir which then gradually releases its accumulated waters during the long, hot months of the dry season. Dotted with stilt villages and floating communities of fishermen, it provides a convenient and fascinating waterway between Phnom Penh and Angkor.

National Assembly building, Phnom Penh

The land

Almost exactly twice the size of Portugal and with a similar population, Cambodia is relatively flat and low-lying. In southwest Indochina, it has a total area of just over 180,000sq km (69,500sq miles). It shares land borders with Laos to the northeast, Vietnam to the east and Thailand to the north and west. Cambodia also has a 443km (277-mile) coastline on the Gulf of Thailand in the southwest. Capital Phnom Penh lies in the southeast.

Two major water features, the Tonlé Sap (Great Lake) and the Mekong River, dominate Cambodia's landscape. The Tonlé Sap is a vast lake in Cambodia's central northwest, surrounded by a fertile plain. The Sap River runs from the lake's southeast end to join the Mekong in Phnom Penh, some 100km (62 miles) distant. The Mekong enters from Laos in the north. It flows in a southerly direction for around 500km (311 miles), up to 5km (3 miles) wide in places, before passing into Vietnam on its way to the South China Sea. The river divides at Phnom Penh. The broader northern branch retains the name Mekong, while the southern branch is known as the Bassac.

Beyond the Mekong-Tonlé Sap Basin, Cambodia is ringed first by plains, most of which are less than 100m (328ft) in elevation, and then by several mountain ranges on the borders of the country. The northern border with Thailand is marked by the Dangrek Mountains, a 350km (217-mile) range of south-facing cliffs rising 180 to 550m (591 to 1,804ft) above the Cambodian plain. In the southwest, covering much of the region between the Tonlé Sap and the Gulf of Thailand, two separate ranges, the Kravanh (Cardamom Mountains) and the Dâmrei (Elephant Mountains), form remote upland areas. It is here that Cambodia's highest peak, Mount Aural at 1,813m (5,948ft), is found.

In the northeast of the country, occupying the remote provinces of Ratanakiri and Mondulkiri, the eastern highlands rise from the plains. This region of thickly forested hills stretches east across the border into Vietnam, and north into neighbouring Laos. Most Cambodians live in small villages in the Mekong and Tonlé Sap regions, and practise subsistence wet-rice cultivation. The annual inundation of the Mekong and Tonlé Sap brings with it rich alluvial silt which makes for fertile soils throughout much of the central plains.

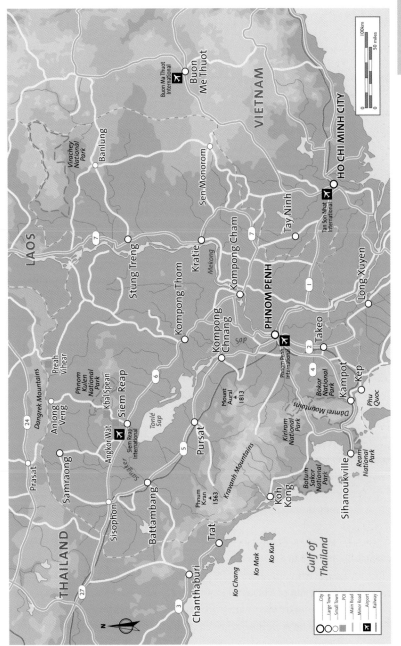

History

Circa 4000 BC Evidence of cave dwellers in northwest Cambodia.

AD 100–600 A trading state called Funan is established in the fertile Mekong Delta. It serves as a port for Arab, Chinese and Indian shipping and also acts as a channel by which Indian religious traditions, especially Hinduism and Buddhism, enter the region.

500–700 An early Khmer state is established inland near the confluence of the Mekong and Sap Rivers. The people of this new state speak a Mon-Khmer language and worship Shiva. The first monumental Khmer architecture is created during the reign of Isanavarman I (616–65) at Sambor Prei Kuk.

802–50 After proclaiming himself a God King, Jayavarman II moves the capital to Roluos near Angkor.

877–89 Indravarman I unifies the Khmer Empire and starts the construction of a huge irrigation system to strengthen the rapidly expanding state.

889–908 During the reign of Yasovarman the capital moves from Roluos to Angkor.

1113–50 The construction of Angkor Wat is completed by Surayavarman II, who also conquers parts of neighbouring Champa to the east.

1177 The Cham sack Angkor.

1181–1215 The influence of Buddhism becomes more apparent under the rule of Jayavarman VII. He constructs the Bayon temple at Angkor Thom and defeats the Cham.

1297–8 A Chinese visitor, Chou Ta Kuan, writes his classic account of life and society in the Kingdom of Angkor.

1352–1430 The Siamese Kingdom of Ayutthaya attacks Angkor on four separate occasions, taking away many prisoners and the symbols of the Khmer court.

1432 After more pressure from the Siamese, the Khmer King Ponhea Yat abandons Angkor and moves his capital to Lovek in the Phnom Penh region.

1593–4	King Naresuan of Siam captures Lovek.
1618–1866	Chey Chettha II moves the capital to Udong.
1859	French land at Saigon.
1862	French make Cochin China a colony.
1863	Under French pressure King Norodom signs a treaty making Cambodia a French protectorate with the king effectively becoming a puppet ruler.
1866	Phnom Penh established as the new capital.
1892	The French seize control of the northwest provinces of Cambodia from Siam. A period of tension follows with some fighting between France and Siam, eventually resulting in the imposition, by France, of the current Thai–Cambodia frontier in 1907.
1941	Thailand invades northwestern Cambodia and reoccupies areas around Battambang and Siem Reap.
1942	King Monivong dies. His successor, Norodom Sihanouk, becomes King of Cambodia.
1945	With Japanese support King Sihanouk declares Cambodian independence.
1946	Following ally Japan's World War II defeat, the Thais are expelled from the country.
1953	France grants Cambodia full independence.
1954	Following the Geneva Conference, France withdraws from the whole of Indochina.
1955	King Sihanouk abdicates and asks his father, Suramarit, to take the throne. In reality Sihanouk retains real power himself.
1960	Cambodia increasingly favours North Vietnam over the United States in the Second Indochina War. Sihanouk becomes more autocratic.
1962	After the disappearance of Tou Samouth, the Cambodian Communist Party leader, Pol Pot takes over the party, and plots a peasant revolt.
1965	The United States escalates the war in Vietnam. Sihanouk

History

breaks off relations with the United States, while continuing to battle local communists.

1967 Cambodian communists under the leadership of Pol Pot – nicknamed 'Khmer Rouge' by Sihanouk – stage a rising in northwest Cambodia. The Cambodian government brutally represses the rebellion.

1969 Clandestine bombing raids by US B-52s on North Vietnamese sanctuaries in Cambodia begin.

1970 Right-wing Cambodian General Lon Nol launches a coup while Sihanouk is abroad for medical reasons. He is deposed and flees to Beijing, and the Khmer Rouge leadership, along with many other leftists, take refuge in the jungle. The US secretly carpet bombs central and eastern Cambodia.

1973 The United States begins its withdrawal of troops from Vietnam, but in Cambodia B-52 carpet bombing continues unabated. In seven months, 250,000 tonnes of bombs are dropped on the countryside.

1975 Phnom Penh falls to the Khmer Rouge on 17 April and orders are immediately given to evacuate all towns. The population is forced into the countryside in an attempt to establish a totally rural-based society. Buddhists and ethnic minorities are brutally suppressed.

1976–8 Mass starvation occurs in northwest Cambodia, following the evacuation of urban dwellers to the area. A wave of anti-Vietnamese militarism leads to conflict with Vietnam. The Khmer Rouge regime is characterised by religious intolerance, national bigotry and widespread mass murder which becomes known as auto-genocide.

1977 In an attempt to eliminate all dissidents, Pol Pot orders a wave of bloody purges. The Khmer Rouge initiates attacks across all three of the country's borders, slaughtering civilians in Laos, Thailand and Vietnam.

1978 More purges occur in the Eastern Zone, sparking an uprising. The rebels are defeated and cross into Vietnam seeking help from Hanoi.

1979 Vietnamese forces invade and overthrow the Khmer Rouge. Eastern Zone rebel leader Heng Samrin is made President, with Hun Sen as Foreign Minister. Pol Pot and other Khmer Rouge leaders flee to the Thai border.

1979–88 The Vietnamese occupy Cambodia with up to 100,000 troops stationed there at any one time. Thailand, China and much of the West support the disgraced Khmer Rouge and its allies.

1989 In September, Vietnamese forces begin their withdrawal from the country.

1991 Sihanouk returns to Phnom Penh.

1993 A general election is held under the direction of the United Nations. Hun Sen's People's Party forms a coalition government with the FUNCINPEC Party of Prince Norodom Ranariddh.

1996 In return for an amnesty, Khmer Rouge deputy leader Ieng Sary defects to the government side.

1998 Pol Pot dies in his jungle hideout near Anlong Veng, possibly committing suicide. The Khmer Rouge finally collapses and in a bid to promote national unity its leaders are offered amnesty.

1999 Cambodia joins the Association of Southeast Asian Nations (ASEAN).

2003 The Cambodian People's Party wins the general election, with Hun Sen remaining in charge.

2004 Due to ill health King Sihanouk abdicates. His son, Norodom Sihamoni, ascends to the throne.

2005 The UN approves a war crimes tribunal set up to try Khmer Rouge leaders.

2007 The Cambodia Genocide Tribunal holds its first public hearings.

2008 Nuon Chea, the most senior surviving Khmer Rouge leader, appears in court for the first time and is refused bail. Other KR leaders, including Ieng Sary, his wife Ieng Thirith, and former Tuol Sleng commandant Kang Kek Iew are similarly remanded in custody and refused bail.

Politics

In May 1993, following the elections organised under the direction of the United Nations, Cambodia officially became a constitutional monarchy with King Norodom Sihanouk as Head of State. The Khmer Rouge guerrillas chose not to take part in the elections, and this led to several more years of sporadic warfare during which the Khmer Rouge was gradually worn down by military pressure.

Pol Pot died – or committed suicide – in 1998, whilst the last Khmer Rouge diehard, military leader Ta Mok, was captured near Anlong Veng in the north of Cambodia and taken to prison in Phnom Penh in 1999. In the same year Kang Kek Iew, better known as 'Comrade Duch', the dreaded former commander of Tuol Sleng Prison, who had overseen the execution of some 20,000 people, was discovered working with a Western NGO in Battambang Province. By now a born-again Christian, Duch has admitted his guilt and is currently on trial in Phnom Penh. Four further senior Khmer Rouge leaders, Pol Pot's 'Brother No 2' Nuon Chea, the former Foreign Minister Ieng Sary with his wife Ieng Thirith, and the former Khmer Rouge President Khieu Samphan, were all arrested in 2007 and are currently on trial at the Cambodia Genocide Tribunal in Phnom Penh.

Following the 1993 elections, Prince Norodom Ranariddh became First Prime Minister, whilst the head of the former Vietnamese-backed regime, Hun Sen, became Second Prime Minister in a power-sharing arrangement that soon broke down. In July 1997, Hun Sen moved against Ranariddh with a swift coup d'état in Phnom Penh that forced the hapless prince to take refuge in France. As a consequence, Hun Sen emerged as the strongman of Cambodian politics. The world reacted with hostility and more than a degree of hypocrisy to these events. Cambodia's long-anticipated admission to ASEAN was postponed (although military-ruled Burma was admitted), and elements in the Cambodian opposition, notably outspoken politician Sam Rainsy, stirred up anti-Vietnamese sentiment in an attempt to weaken the Hun Sen government. Today Hun Sen remains very much in charge of the country.

The Cambodian economy has been virtually destroyed twice in recent decades: first when the Khmer Rouge entered Phnom Penh in 1975, and again with the 1989 withdrawal of Vietnamese troops and the collapse of their Soviet paymasters, a major source of aid. Over the past decade, however, matters have gradually improved. The greatest sources of foreign revenue are timber and gem exports, foreign aid and garment manufacture for overseas markets. Cambodia is starting to see some foreign investment in the services sector, while the tourist industry grows more important every year. The situation is improving, but more investment is needed in education, basic infrastructure and telecommunications before Cambodia will start to look truly attractive to foreign investors.

Economic growth remains steady at around 5 per cent. Tourism, which promises to be Cambodia's most reliable and sustainable source of foreign exchange, is the country's fastest growing industry, with arrivals growing from 220,000 in 1997 to more than two million in 2007. As more temple complexes are opened and the coastal strip is developed for tourism, these figures can only increase.

Pol Pot in the jungle – Khmer Rouge propaganda picture

Culture

The most distinctive and enduring aspect of Cambodian culture is Buddhism. Most Cambodians – around 90 per cent of the population – are Buddhists. As in Thailand and Laos they are followers of the Theravada school, or 'Way of the Elders'. In contrast, the form of Buddhism followed in neighbouring Vietnam is Mahayana, as in China, Korea and Japan. This distinction reinforces the already deep cultural and social differences between Cambodians and Vietnamese.

Buddhism gradually spread throughout Cambodia from the 10th century, over time replacing Hinduism as the state religion. Theravada Buddhism teaches personal salvation through the way of the Noble Eightfold Path. The eight constituents are right understanding, right motive, right speech, right action, right livelihood, right effort, right mindfulness and right contemplation. The central core of Buddhist belief lies in the Four Noble Truths taught by the Buddha, which are *Dukkha*, or that there can be no existence without suffering; *Samudaya*, or that the cause of suffering is egoistic desire; *Nirodha*, or that the elimination of desire extinguishes suffering; and finally *Magga*, or that the way to extinguish suffering is the Noble Eightfold Path.

The ultimate goal of Theravada Buddhism is Nirvana, or 'extinction'. In essence this means an end to corporeal existence and to the endless cycle of rebirth. Most Cambodians, however, aim simply to achieve a better rebirth.

This can be attained by accruing good *karma* and avoiding bad *karma*. Simple and effective ways of achieving this are abstaining from taking life, refraining from intoxicants, gambling and sexual promiscuity, keeping calm and not getting angry, respecting the elderly and so on. A very popular way of earning merit is to give donations to temples and monks, whether this be the expensive construction of a stupa or the simple donation of some food to an itinerant monk.

Above all, honour and respect should be paid to the *triratana*, or 'Three Jewels' of Buddha, *sangha* (order of monks) and *dhamma* (sacred teachings). In consequence, nearly all Cambodian Buddhist men will join the *sangha* and become monks at least once in their lives. Women, too, may become ordained as nuns, though the percentage is lower and the decision is generally delayed until middle or old age when the task of raising children has been completed. Buddhism, like other religions, suffered terribly under the Khmer Rouge, but today it is making a major comeback.

Cambodia's second religion is Islam. Nearly all Muslims are ethnic Cham, at around 550,000 people the country's second largest minority after the Vietnamese. Originally refugees from 18th-century Vietnam, the Cham practise a rather relaxed form of Sunni Islam, fasting one day a week during the month of Ramadan, abstaining from pork but often drinking alcohol. Since the time of the Khmer Rouge, when Muslims suffered greatly, aid in the form of money, new mosques, books and education from Malaysia

and the Middle East is gradually resulting in the establishment of an orthodox Sunni Muslim tradition.

Christianity, introduced to Indochina by the French, never made much headway amongst the Buddhist Khmers. The Vietnamese, by contrast, were much more open to new religions, and several million converted to Catholicism. Because of this, Christianity in Cambodia is closely associated with Vietnamese. This may be one reason why the viscerally anti-Vietnamese Khmer Rouge completely destroyed Phnom Penh Cathedral. Today Christian missionaries are once again working in Cambodia, but

Traditional dancers accept the applause after a performance

indigenous Christians remain few on the ground.

At more than one million people, ethnic Vietnamese constitute the largest minority in Cambodia. They include representatives of all Vietnamese religious persuasions, from Mahayana Buddhism, through Confucianism, to Taoism, as well as other Vietnamese faiths such as the Cao Dai and Hoa Hao sects. The Holy See of the Cao Dai is in the Vietnamese province of Tay Ninh, close to the Cambodian frontier, and this syncretic religion – which counts Victor Hugo, Laozi and Jesus among its saints – has also won some Khmer converts.

Animism in Cambodia is generally limited to hill peoples, known as *Khmer Loeu*, including the Kuy, Mnong, Brao and Jarai of Mondulkiri and Ratanakiri Provinces, and the Pear and Saoch of

Children and gods at the South Gate of Angkor Thom

the Cardamom and Elephant Mountains. As in nearby Thailand, the spirit world is also very important to Cambodian Buddhists. Spirit houses are a frequent sight in Khmer homes, and locality spirits are widely believed in across the country.

Music

There are two types of traditional orchestra in Cambodia, the all-male *pip hat* and the all-female *mohori*. Both employ 11 traditional musical instruments. These include stringed instruments, flutes, gongs, xylophones and three-stringed guitars. Music is sometimes accompanied by song, either improvised ballads or more usually formal court chants. At some festivals a traditional orchestra known as *phleng pinpeat* will give performances of royal court music. Another type of orchestra is the *phleng khmer*, which usually performs at weddings. Popular music has been strongly influenced in recent years by both Thai and Chinese pop culture, and Western pop music is increasingly to be heard in Phnom Penh and other large towns.

Literature

As in other Indian-influenced countries, traditional Cambodian literature revolves around the great Hindu epic *Ramayana*, known in its Khmer version as the *Reamker*. This is the story of Prince Rama, an incarnation of Vishnu, and his wife Sita, who is kidnapped by Ravana, the demon-king of Lanka. The story is more than 2,000 years old, and figures prominently both in the bas-reliefs at Angkor Wat and in the much newer murals at the Royal Palace in Phnom Penh. The *Reamker* is also the main inspirational source for traditional theatrical performances including those of the Royal Theatre.

Dance

The Cambodian Royal Ballet suffered particularly badly under the Khmer Rouge, which attempted, almost successfully, to destroy the tradition completely. Fortunately, a handful of dancers survived, as did its principal ballerina Princess Bupphadevi, a daughter of King Sihanouk, who was living in France. In the three decades since the fall of the Khmer Rouge the Royal Ballet has been painstakingly rebuilt, and today regular performances can be seen in Phnom Penh and Siem Reap. Classical Khmer dance, or *lamthon*, as performed by the Royal Ballet, bears a striking resemblance to that of the Thai royal court, and indeed the two traditions influenced each other in turn until they became practically a shared art form. Training takes many years, and sumptuously elaborate costumes and headdresses are worn. Interestingly, Cambodian masked theatre, known as *khaul*, is also very similar to the Thai *khon*. Classical dances are often performed depicting incidents from the Buddha birth cycle stories, or *Jataka*.

Festivals and events

Festivals form an important part of Cambodia's calendar, although not all are public holidays. This is a selection of the most important festivals celebrated either throughout the country or in specific locations. Note that festivals are often accompanied by feasts and raucous get-togethers. Many of Cambodia's most important events are based on the lunar calendar so the specific date varies from year to year.

January/February
Chaul Chnam Chen (Chinese and Vietnamese New Year)
There are sizeable Chinese and Vietnamese communities in Phnom Penh and other large cities. Although firecrackers are now banned in Vietnam for safety reasons, it is still possible to observe (and hear) this spectacle in Vietnamese neighbourhoods of Cambodia.
Late January/early February

Meak Bochea (Big Prayer)
This is one of the most important Buddhist holidays of the year and is held to commemorate the gathering of 1,250 disciples to witness the Buddha's last sermon. Candlelit processions take place at temples around the country.
January/February full moon

April
Chaul Chnam (Cambodian New Year)
Water is flung everywhere in celebration of a new year, and similar events occur in neighbouring Laos, Thailand and Myanmar. Offerings are made at temples and small sand *chedis* are built in the temple compounds as representations of Mount Meru. Houses are cleaned methodically in a gesture of renewal.
13–15 April

May
Bon Choat Preah Nengkal (Ploughing of the Holy Furrow)
This old Hindu ceremony marks the beginning of the rice-planting season. Sacred bulls are offered different foods to eat by Royal Brahmin priests and, depending on the animals' choice, seers predict the coming harvest.
Mid to late May, Phnom Penh

Visakha Bochea (Buddha's birthday)
This is the most important of all Buddhist holy days and commemorates the Buddha's birth, enlightenment and entry into Nirvana. It's accompanied by candlelit parades around temples.
May full moon

July
Chol Vassa (Buddhist Lent)

A traditional period for young Cambodian men to join the monkhood. Formerly most men taking vows for the first time would spend the whole of the rainy season in the temple, but these days it is more customary to spend only two, maybe three, weeks there.

September/October
Bon Pchum Ben (Spirit Commemoration Festival)

Respects are paid to ancestors through offerings at temples all over the country in what is a Cambodian equivalent of All Souls' Day.

Late September/early October full moon

October/November
Bon Om Tuk (Water Festival)

To celebrate the beginning of the cool season boat races are held on rivers, and monks at temples around the country will row ceremonial boats. The best boat races occur in Phnom Penh on the Sap River.

October/November full moon

November
Independence Day

Events in Phnom Penh usually begin with an early morning ceremony at the Independence Monument. Other celebrations include an elaborate parade in front of the Royal Palace and fireworks on the riverfront in the evening.

9 November

November/December/January
Angkor Festival

The temples of Angkor serve as a magnificent backdrop for a series of traditional arts presentations by performers from various Asian countries. Arts include poetry, traditional dance, folk music and exhibitions of national cuisine.

The Royal Palace at Phnom Penh is at the heart of the celebrations of Independence Day

Highlights

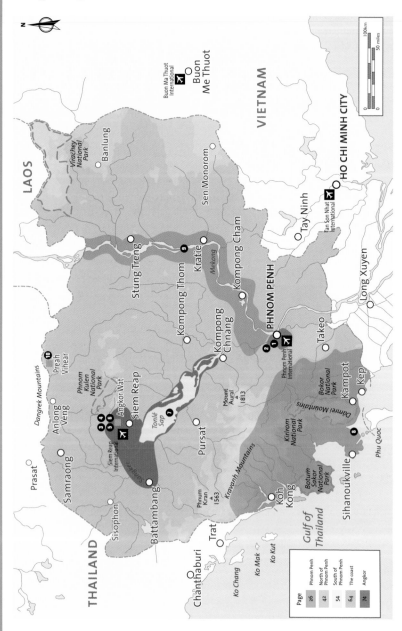

Page	
26	Phnom Penh
42	North of Phnom Penh
54	South of Phnom Penh
64	The coast
74	Angkor

1 Preah Barom Reachea Vaeng Chaktomuk (Royal Palace)

Located in the heart of Phnom Penh by the junction of the Sap and Mekong Rivers, this is the splendid official residence of Cambodia's kings and the site of the Royal Throne Hall and Wat Preah Keo, or Silver Pagoda as visitors call it (*see pp29–31*).

2 Saramohnti Cheat (National Museum)

Behind the Royal Palace in central Phnom Penh, the museum is housed in attractive, red brick pavilions and courtyards displaying the finest collection of Cambodian art and sculpture in the country (*see pp31, 34–5*).

3 Angkor Wat

The 'City which is a Temple' is the single largest religious complex anywhere in the world. Nowhere else on earth, except maybe in the Valley of the Nile in Egypt, are the relics of antiquity found on so monumental a scale (*see pp84–9*).

4 The Bayon

Built in the late 12th century by the Buddhist King Jayavarman VII, the Bayon is chiefly celebrated for the vast, serene stone heads that distinguish the structure and are said to be carved in the likeness of Jayavarman VII himself (*see pp90–91*).

5 Ta Prohm

Also built in the 12th century by the industrious Jayavarman VII, this magnificent jungle-covered temple, deliberately left in its original, semi-abandoned state, smothered by the roots of great kapok and strangling fig trees, was made famous in the movie *Tomb Raider* (*see pp112–13*).

6 Kbal Spean

The 'River of a Thousand Linga' gets its name from the hundreds of fertility symbols carved into the rock sides and bed of the Kbal Spean River that flows down from the mountains to the north of Angkor to water the surrounding plains (*see pp118–19*).

7 Tonlé Sap

The great freshwater lake that dominates northwest Cambodia is justly celebrated for its extraordinary fertility, floating rice, rich fish stocks, fishing boats and itinerant floating village communities (*see pp79–81*).

8 The south coast beaches

The beaches between Sihanoukville and Kep are lush and pristine but nowhere near as developed as comparable strands in neighbouring Thailand or Vietnam – a major part of their appeal (*see pp66–9*).

9 The Mekong River
Running through the heart of the country, it is vast, serene and redolent with history. Take a boat trip through Cambodia's mystical 'heart of darkness' and marvel at the solitude and fascinating wildlife (*see pp48–9*).

10 Preah Vihear temple
Perched on an all but inaccessible cliff top in the Dangrek Mountains on the Thai border, the temple symbolises both Cambodia's past glory and the territories it has lost to acquisitive neighbours over the centuries (*see pp52–3*).

Ta Prohm, between Angkor Wat and Angkor Thom

Suggested itineraries

These itineraries will let you see as much of the destination as time allows. They are admittedly fast-paced, and each individual will of course have special interests and choose to focus more on some areas or types of sights longer than, or to the exclusion of, others. Where time is short, taxis and planes are recommended; if you have more time or wish to economise, substitute walking and bus journeys where appropriate.

Long weekends

On such a flying visit, it's best to stay in and around Phnom Penh. Spend a day exploring the Sap River front, from venerable Wat Phnom in the north, via Sisowath Quay and its many open-air restaurants, to the Royal Palace and the Silver Pagoda. The National Museum is best seen in the afternoon, especially if it's raining. In the evening enjoy a cold drink at the Foreign Correspondents Club of Cambodia while watching the sun set over the junction of the Sap and Mekong Rivers.

You're likely to want to fit in some shopping. Depending on your wish list, choose from: Psar Thmei, the spectacular Art Deco Central Market, for its gold and souvenir stalls; O Russei for fresh vegetables, flowers and local products; Psar Olympic for perfumes, liquors and better quality clothing; and Psar Tuol Tom Pong's curio and antique stalls.

Follow dinner at one of the fine restaurants overlooking the Sap River with a late evening stroll along Sisowath Quay, where there are numerous pubs and watering holes. If you are looking for night-time entertainment, the bustling nocturnal scene is at its most vibrant at Street 51 south of Psar Thmei market.

On a more sobering note, visit Tuol Sleng Genocide Museum and the 'Killing Fields' of Choeung Ek, both located to the south of town. For something cheerier, celebrate Cambodia's cultural revival by watching a performance at the Royal Ballet. To pack in as much as possible, make use of the local cabs and *motos* (motorbike taxis) to get from one place to another.

One-week trips

A week allows you to venture outside the capital and see Angkor, the essence of any visit to Cambodia. Apart from a few days in Phnom Penh, you'll probably want to base yourself in Siem Reap, to which it's best to fly. Eat out on Bar Street where there are plenty of good restaurants serving a choice of Cambodian, Thai, Vietnamese, French and Italian cuisine. Nightlife here is pretty quiet, but this doesn't matter as you'll need your energy for daytime explorations of the amazing nearby temple complex at Angkor.

The most convenient option is to hire a cab for the full length of your stay in Siem Reap, asking the driver to collect you in the mornings, driving you back to town for lunch and a siesta before heading out, once again, to the temples in the afternoon and early evening. Buy a three-day entrance ticket at the Angkor entrance booth and take good care of it – checks are frequent and serious.

The French divided the Angkor experience into the Small and Large Circuits, and this distinction still makes sense today. It's best to visit Angkor Thom in the morning, leaving Angkor Wat for the afternoon and evening when the setting sun shows the temple at its best. On the Large Circuit visit Preah Khan temple, continuing via Neak Pean and the East Mebon. Follow in the footsteps of the explorer Henri Mouhot and the actress Angelina Jolie to see the unbelievably atmospheric Ta Prohm temple and also visit nearby Banteay Kdei. Banteay Srei or 'Citadel of Women', an exquisite pink sandstone temple set amid sugar palms and rice fields some 30km (18½ miles) northeast of Siem Reap, is best seen early in the morning to avoid the crowds. En route it's possible to stop and visit one of several traditional Khmer farming villages where you can see palm sugar and coconut toddy being made, and you will have an opportunity to purchase locally made handicrafts at very reasonable prices.

Two-week trips

Cambodia is a relatively small country, so two weeks is plenty of time to see a lot without rushing too much. From

A common rural scene in central Cambodia

Fishermen on the lake, Tonlé Sap

the capital, take the fast river boat to Siem Reap via Tonlé Sap, a five-hour journey through floating fishing communities and stilt villages. Explore Angkor at your leisure – even with a seven-day ticket there's a lot to see. Hike up into the mountains north of Angkor to visit the forest sanctuary of Kbal Spean and the Kulen Mountains. Explore the older Roluos group of temples, predating Angkor by several centuries, about 12km (7½ miles) east of Siem Reap. In the evening, watch an *apsara* dance performance at one of several venues in town. The Raffles show is particularly good, but it's not cheap, and requires booking in advance. From Siem Reap, visit the floating village on the Tonlé Sap by Phnom Krom.

Longer visits

Once you have explored Phnom Penh and Angkor, head south to the coast between Sihanoukville and Kep and just lie back and relax on the unspoiled and still relatively tourist-free beaches. If you're feeling adventurous, take a diving trip from Sihanoukville, or a boat trip up the coast to Koh Kong, a frontier town next to Thailand with a distinctly 'wild west' feel to it that thrives on gambling and nightlife. Alternatively, take a flight from Phnom Penh to Ratanakiri Province in Cambodia's remote northeast, once home to guerrillas and bandits but now distinguished by some of the most pristine natural scenery in the country. Visit beautiful Yak Loum Crater Lake before taking a car or bus west along Highway 19 to the isolated rubber-producing town of Stung Treng on the east bank of the Mekong. Spend a morning watching the friendly Irrawaddy dolphins at play, then take the river express downstream to Phnom Penh, perhaps stopping to visit the isolated town of Kratie and the historic city of Kompong Cham en route.

Phnom Penh

Phnom Penh, the Cambodian capital, is an attractive riverside city of just over two million people, characterised by broad boulevards and with plenty of sights to interest the visitor. All of the more important attractions are located next to, or within walking distance of, the Phnom Penh riverside, an area which also has many of the best restaurants, bars and cafés in town.

Despite being badly run down following three decades of war, the city retains considerable Cambodian and colonial charm. French villas and tree-lined boulevards remind the visitor that Phnom Penh was once considered a gem amongst Indochinese cities. Double-digit economic growth rates in recent years have resulted in an economic boom, with new hotels, cafés, residential buildings and even the first few high-rise towers springing up across the city. The numerous historical and cultural sites include the Royal Palace and Silver Pagoda, the distinguished National Museum, Wat Phnom, Wat Ounalom and other temples, a number of bustling markets including the unusual Art Deco Central Market and some fine colonial architecture, much already restored. Tuol Sleng and the infamous 'Killing Fields' of Choeung Ek are grim reminders of the former Khmer Rouge regime (1975–9).

Chatomuk

Phnom Penh was previously known as *Krong Chatomuk* meaning 'City of Four Faces', a reference to the very centre of town where the Mekong River – so broad at this point that it is difficult to see across – meets the Sap and Bassac Rivers. The best way to see Chatomuk is to walk south along Sisowath Quay, the riverside drive that hugs the west bank of the Sap River, to the latter's junction with the Mekong. The area is always busy with sightseers and vendors, and both the Sap and Mekong Rivers are generally dotted with small fishing boats, as well as larger vessels making their way upstream to Phnom Penh river port and beyond, or downstream to Vietnam and the open waters of the South China Sea.

As well as offering fascinating and beautiful views, Chatomuk is remarkable for a unique phenomenon: the reversal of the Sap River. From May to October, during the annual rainy season, the hugely increased volume of the Mekong forces the Sap River to back up, and finally reverse its course, flowing northwards to flood the Tonlé Sap with vast quantities of fresh water and rich sediment (*see box on p79*).

The time of the October reversal of the waters is celebrated as *Bon Om Tuk*, one of Cambodia's most important festivals. If you are lucky enough to be in Phnom Penh at this time, then Chatomuk is the place to be – though you will have to share the scene with thousands of other spectators and merry-makers.

The area around Chatomuk lies at the heart of royal Phnom Penh. Attractions in this area include the Royal Palace, the Silver Pagoda and the National Museum. It is also rewarding to take a short river cruise by day or a dinner cruise in the evening. Most cruises last between one and two hours, leaving from the quay between Street 178 and Street 130 and running down

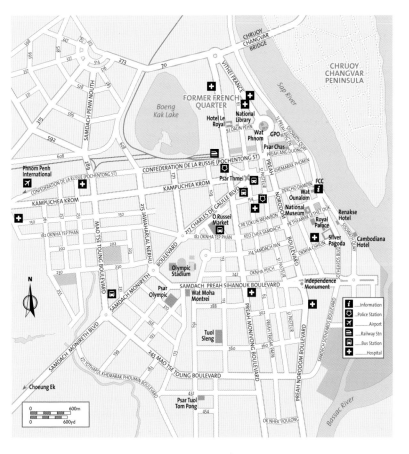

the Sap River past the Royal Palace to the Mekong, turning upstream to see the nearby 'floating villages' before returning to the point of departure.

Photography is best in the early morning as the rising sun illuminates the Royal Palace and the surrounding Phnom Penh skyline.

General Post Office, former French Quarter, Phnom Penh

To the east of the Cambodiana Hotel, Sisowath Quay. Most boats are private charters, but the Kanika catamaran does regular trips at 4–6pm & 6–9pm (with dinner).

The former French Quarter

Along Street 47 (also known as Vithei France) and its smaller side streets, stand numerous dilapidated old colonial buildings, many of which have been or are being renovated. This is the old French Quarter, characterised by ochre yellow and sky blue paintwork, French-style window shutters and some elaborate colonial stucco work. Many of the city's embassies are located in this area in some of the grandest old colonial buildings. Fine examples of restored colonial architecture are to be found at the General Post Office on Street 13, the National Library on Street 92 and the Hotel Le Royal, also on Street 92 – but the best way to get a feel for this historic area is to stroll north along Street 47, making forays into the numerous side streets, before returning south along Preah Monivong Boulevard.

To the north and east of Wat Phnom.

Preah Barom Reachea Vaeng Chaktomuk (Royal Palace)

Just south of the National Museum lie the grounds of the Royal Palace, built in Khmer style from the middle of the 19th century after the old royal capital was moved from Udong to the north of Phnom Penh. It was constructed, with French assistance, on the site of an old

THE FOREIGN CORRESPONDENTS CLUB OF CAMBODIA

The FCC (as it is generally known) is a Phnom Penh institution – and despite its name it's open to everyone, and not just journalists. Located in the heart of the city, overlooking the Sap River and the Chatomuk, it's housed in a lovingly restored three-storey French colonial building that offers wonderful views of the river junction and Sisowath Quay below. As well as a fine restaurant and bar offering international and Khmer cuisine, the FCC houses a bookstore selling literature relating to Cambodia and Indochina, and holds occasional exhibitions of Indochina-themed photography as well as book launches and other media activities.

citadel called Banteay Kev, facing east towards the rising sun and the nearby Chatomuk.

The palace functions as the official residence of the formally retired 'King Father' Norodom Sihanouk and, more recently, King Norodom Sihamoni, who succeeded to the throne on his father's retirement in 2004. The main entrance is in the east of the palace grounds, opposite the colonial-style Renakse Hotel. Guide pamphlets are available near the ticket office, and guided tours are both available and recommended.

Some areas within the palace, including the king's residential quarters, are off limits to the public, but most of the complex is accessible. The **Chan Chhaya Pavilion**, formerly used by Cambodian kings to review parades and hold performances of classical Khmer dancing, stands just beyond the entrance gate.

Overlooking the centre of the larger, northern section of the royal grounds is the **Royal Throne Hall**. This was built in 1917, the architect borrowing extensively from the Bayon Period style at Angkor. The cruciform building is crowned with three spires. The central one is topped with a white, four-faced head of the Hindu god Brahma. Inside, the Throne Hall contains a royal throne and busts of past Cambodian kings. The ceiling is adorned with murals from the *Reamker*, the Khmer adaptation of the *Ramayana*. Apart from coronations, the Throne Hall is used for significant constitutional events and for the acceptance of ambassadorial credentials. Photography is forbidden inside.

To the northwest of the Throne Hall stands the restricted Royal Residence Compound called the **Khemarin Palace**, whilst to the south are several buildings, including the **Royal Treasury**, housing the regalia used in royal coronation ceremonies including the Great Crown of Victory, the Victory Spear and the Sacred Sword.

Nearby stand the **Royal Banqueting Hall** and the **Napoleon III Pavilion**. This latter building was initially given by the Emperor Napoleon III to his wife the Empress Eugénie, who in turn had it taken apart and sent to Phnom Penh as a present for King Norodom in the 1870s. The pavilion functions as a museum of royal memorabilia including busts, portraits, gifts from foreign ambassadors, elaborate silk clothing, porcelain, glass and all manner of regal knick-knacks. Unfortunately, the exterior of the structure is currently in need of significant restoration.

A recent addition to the palace complex, located near the main

Fishing boats near the confluence of the Sap and Mekong Rivers, Phnom Penh

Napoleon III Pavilion at the Royal Palace

entrance and exit gate, is a small display hall devoted to the recent coronation of King Norodom Sihamoni. A large glass case contains a lifelike reconstruction of the king being borne aloft in an elaborate palanquin on the shoulders of his courtiers.

Samdech Sothearos Boulevard.
Open: daily 7.30–11am & 2–5pm.
Admission charge.

Saramohnti Cheat (National Museum)

Housed in a splendid red pavilion, the museum contains a magnificent collection of Khmer art including some of the best pieces in existence. It also 'houses' an estimated two million bats, which explains the sharp, acrid smell and the constant squeaking and twittering from above the specially strengthened ceiling. It's a good idea to purchase a copy of the museum guidebook, *Khmer Art in Stone*, for US$3 at the entrance desk.

The museum building was originally constructed in Cambodian style under the supervision of the French archaeologist and academic George Groslier (1887–1945), who became the museum's first director. Four covered *(cont. on p34)*

Walk: Phnom Penh riverside

Many of Phnom Penh's most interesting sights are to be found along the right bank of the Sap River between Wat Phnom in the north and Chatomuk in the south. En route are many small riverside cafés and restaurants serving a wide selection of cuisines both al fresco and – in the rainy season or in the heat of the afternoon sun – indoors, generally with air-conditioning. There are many small bars, too, serving cold drinks all day long.

Allow two hours for this 2km (1¼-mile) walk, longer if you intend to visit the Royal Palace or other attractions en route.
Start in the north at Wat Phnom and continue southeast along the riverfront.

1 Sisowath Quay

Once very rundown and shabby, this entire area has been beautified in recent years, with pleasant lawns and a paved footpath running above the restored breakwater; a long row of flagpoles bearing the flags of many countries lines the path, and there are numerous benches and other places to sit. On the far side of the Sap River the Chruoy Changvar Peninsula is green and relatively undeveloped, the location of several fine seafood restaurants and a popular picnic spot for locals. The multi-coloured Buddhist flag of Wat Sampeuv Meas is clearly visible in the near distance. The restaurants by Sisowath Quay are an excellent place to savour the French culinary influence of

Cambodia's colonial past, as well as to breakfast on coffee with fresh, locally made croissants, or baguette and pâté.
Walk south as far as the FCC, then turn right, off Sisowath Quay, onto Samdech Sothearos Boulevard.

2 Wat Ounalom (Eyebrow Temple)

Just behind the FCC stand the headquarters of the Cambodian *sangha*, or Buddhist order. Founded in 1443, this important temple suffered badly at the hands of the Khmer Rouge, but has since been restored. Regrettably, the once extensive library of the Buddhist Institute, which is also found here, will take many years to restore. To the west of the main temple stands a stupa said to contain a hair of the Buddha. Within the temple are several ancient Buddha images vandalised by the Khmer Rouge but since reassembled. Also on display is a statue of Samdech Huot Tat, head of the Cambodian *sangha* when Pol Pot came to power and subsequently killed by the Khmer Rouge. The statue was recovered from the nearby river and reinstalled after the collapse of the Khmer Rouge regime.

Samdech Sotheros Boulevard. Open: daily 6am–6pm. Free admission. Continue south. Turn right and walk west through a small park for about 100m (110yd).

3 Saramohnti Cheat (National Museum)

Housed in a red pavilion dating from 1918, this holds a wonderful collection of Khmer art including some of the finest pieces in existence (*see pp31, 34–5*).

Retrace your steps to Sotheros Boulevard and turn right, continuing south for 80m (90yd).

4 Preah Barom Reachea Vaeng Chaktomuk (Royal Palace)

The official residence of the Cambodian monarchy since 1866, this extensive complex represents the heart of the city and is in large part open to the public (*see pp29–31*). It is important to dress properly and behave in a respectful manner.

Leave the main compound by the southeast gate and continue south for a few metres.

5 Wat Preah Keo (Silver Pagoda)

This structure, so named because its floor is lined with more than 5,000 silver tiles weighing more than 1kg (2.2lb) each, or 5 tonnes in total, is also

known as Wat Preah Keo, or 'Temple of the Emerald Buddha' (*see p41*).

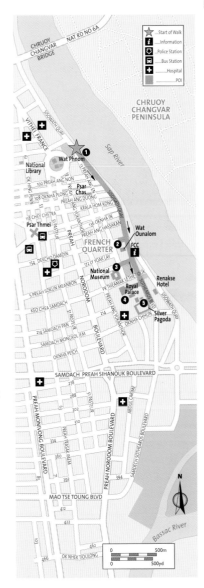

Royal Palace, Phnom Penh

galleries are linked round a spacious central courtyard where Khmer statuary mingles perfectly with tropical plants.

An exploration of the museum begins in the **East Gallery**. Here the highlights include a 10th-century grey sandstone *garuda* from Koh Ker, various bronze artefacts dating back as far as the pre-Angkorean Funan Period (AD c100–600) and bronze images from the Hindu pantheon including the elephant-headed god Ganesh and the bull Nandi, generally represented as the mount of the god Vishnu. A magnificent but sadly incomplete bronze image of Vishnu reclining dominates the far end of the gallery. Recovered from Angkor's West Mebon, it was once 6m (20ft) in length and inlaid with gold.

The **South Gallery** houses more pre-Angkorean statues including a headless image of the goddess Durga from Sambor Prei Kuk. It's unmistakably Indic in design, with broad hips and full breasts. Also displayed here are early images of Vishnu, Krishna and Harihara – the latter a remarkable hybrid of Vishnu and Shiva generally represented as a single head with two distinctly differing sides to the face. The gallery also houses Angkor Period statues including a strikingly female figure of Queen Rajendradevi, a consort of King Jayavarman VII (c1181–1215), the greatest of Angkor's builders.

The **West Gallery** mainly houses sculptures dating from the late 10th century, covering the Angkor Wat and Bayon Periods, including the celebrated

THE ROYAL BALLET

The beauty and elegance of the Cambodian Royal Ballet is legendary. British novelist Somerset Maugham witnessed a performance at Angkor in the 1920s, and wrote that 'the beauty of these dances against the dark mystery of the temple made it the most beautiful and unearthly sight imaginable. It was certainly more than worthwhile to have travelled thousands of miles for.' The dancers had an even greater impact on Auguste Rodin, who exclaimed on seeing a performance in Paris in 1906: 'These Cambodian women have given us everything antiquity could hold. It's impossible to see human nature reaching such perfection. There is only this and the Greeks.'

Tuol Sleng and Choeung Ek

A very different Phnom Penh sight – indeed one that can hardly be called an attraction – is the former Tuol Sleng Prison, now called Tuol Sleng Genocide Museum. Here, during Pol Pot's years in power, around 18,000 people were interrogated under torture and subsequently murdered, generally together with their families.

The former prison, originally a school, is truly a place to chill the soul. Pictures of many of those killed, including women and children, are

Phnom Penh

late 12th-century statue of a cross-legged Jayavarman VII. The **North Gallery** is given over to a collection of post-Angkorean artefacts including a multi-armed bas-relief of the bodhisattva Lokesvara looted from Banteay Chmar Temple in 1998 and subsequently returned to the Cambodian authorities from Thailand, where it had been smuggled for sale.

The **Central Courtyard** is dominated by the famous statue of Yama, God of the Underworld, taken from the 'Terrace of the Leper King' in Angkor Thom (*see p96*). In fact 'Leper King' is a misnomer, applied to the statue because, when found, it was discoloured and covered with growths of lichen and moss.
Streets 178 and 13. Tel: (023) 211 753.
Email: museum_cam@camnet.com.kh.
Open: daily 8am–5pm.
Admission charge.

Cambodian Royal Ballet

starkly displayed in black and white on the museum walls. The primitive instruments of torture and execution employed by the guards are on display, as is a bust of the Khmer Rouge dictator Pol Pot, and a series of paintings by one of the few prisoners to survive. Many of the former classrooms were divided in a very primitive fashion into tiny cells. Everywhere there are crude shackles and old ammunition boxes used as makeshift latrines.

Upon arrival at the prison, inmates were photographed and required to give detailed biographies, from their childhood to the time of their arrest. Next, they were forced to strip to their underwear, and their possessions were confiscated. The prisoners were then taken to their cells. Initially, some of those put to death were people the Khmer Rouge perceived as 'class enemies' and supporters of the former government, but soon the communist regime began to devour itself in a frenzy of suspicion. By the time Tuol Sleng was liberated in 1979, nearly all those suffering torture and execution were Khmer Rouge officials who had fallen under suspicion of being 'KGB-CIA-Vietnamese' agents and who, under severe torture, implicated thousands more of their fellow cadres.

Pictures of victims at Tuol Sleng Genocide Museum, Phnom Penh

There was no escape from Tuol Sleng. All prisoners passing through its gates were destined for torture and death. They were taken to the 'Killing Fields' of Choeung Ek in secret at night, and beaten to death. The only exceptions were 12 prisoners who managed to survive because, in the chaos caused by the Vietnamese seizure of Phnom Penh in December 1979, the prison authorities neglected to execute them.

The speed of the Vietnamese advance also caused the Khmer Rouge to flee without destroying their meticulous prison records, including thousands of photographs and confessions obtained under torture. This unexpected and horrific 'windfall' subsequently enabled

Memorial to victims of Khmer Rouge atrocities, Choeung Ek, Phnom Penh

THE LOST EXECUTIONER

The Director of Tuol Sleng Prison was Kang Kek Iew, better known as 'Comrade Duch'. A senior Khmer Rouge cadre, he was nevertheless not a member of the top ranking leadership, and took his orders from Son Sen (murdered by Pol Pot in 1997) and 'Brother No 2' Nuon Chea, the senior surviving Khmer Rouge leader on trial today. Duch just managed to escape capture by the Vietnamese and fled to the Battambang where – although a dedicated communist until that time – he came under the influence of an American-trained evangelist and became a born-again Christian. This was bad news for the rest of the Khmer Rouge leadership, as when Duch was identified and arrested in 1999, he immediately confessed his guilt and implicated his superiors, beginning with Nuon Chea. In 2007 he was put on trial for genocide in Phnom Penh, and is likely to be the star witness for the prosecution.

the Vietnamese and their Cambodian allies to turn Tuol Sleng from a prison into a museum. The evidence amassed, together with the testimony of 'Comrade Duch', the S21 Director (*see box*), are central to the ongoing trial for genocide of the surviving Khmer Rouge leadership today.

Tuol Sleng is at Street 113 and Street 350. Open: daily 8–11.30am & 2–5.30pm. Admission charge. The 'Killing Fields' of Choeung Ek are 15km (9 miles) south of the capital and can be reached by taxi from Tuol Sleng. Open: daily 8–11.30am & 2–5.30pm. Admission charge.

Walk: Phnom Penh markets

The Cambodian capital has several fascinating and quite different markets that merit a visit. It's relatively easy to walk between them starting at the Old Market in the north and finishing at Tuol Tom Pong in the south, but as an alternative, visitors may prefer to take a taxi or moto between the various locations. The total distance covered is about 4km (2½ miles).

Allow at least half a day for this walk.

1 Psar Chas (Old Market)

The longest-established market in central Phnom Penh is located at the junction of Street 108 and Street 13. It's a very busy, tightly packed bazaar offering a wide selection of pirated tapes and books, clothing, jewellery, dry goods and fresh vegetables. It stays open late into the evening.

Walk west along Street 108, then turn left along Preah Norodom Boulevard. After 200m (220yd) turn right along Street 130.

2 Psar Thmei (Art Deco Market)

This remarkable structure was erected in 1937 during the French colonial period. Built in Art Deco style, its appearance is something like a Babylonian ziggurat. Beneath the dome are numerous gold and silver shops selling locally made jewellery, as well as Khmer *kramaa* (scarves), antiques and other souvenirs.

Walk southwest along Street 217 for 150m (165yd) before turning left onto Preah Monivong Boulevard. Continue south for about 600m (660yd) before turning right along Street 182 for a further 300m (330yd).

3 O Russei Market

Specialities here include more expensive goods, running from perfumes and liquor, through clothing and jewellery, to imported foodstuffs.

Continue west along Street 182 as far as Street 217. Turn left and continue southwest for 750m (825yd) past the Olympic Stadium on your left, as far as the junction with Sihanouk Boulevard. Turn left along Samdach Preah Sihanouk Boulevard for a further 500m (550yd). Turn right up Street 199 for a short distance.

4 Psar Olympic (Olympic Market)

This market is definitely more downmarket than O Russei. Nearly everyone is Cambodian, and the goods on display reflect their requirements for fresh food and flowers. Also well represented are clothes, shoes and bicycles.

Retrace your steps to Samdach Preah Sihanouk Boulevard and turn right, continuing as far as the junction with Street 163. Turn right and continue down Street 163 for 1¼km (¾ mile), crossing Mao Tse Toung Boulevard en route. You may prefer to take a taxi for this final part of the route.

5 Psar Tuol Tom Pong (Russian Market)

This is one of the best places in town to shop for genuine and reproduction antiquities, Buddha figures, silk clothing, silver jewellery and ornaments, gemstones, old money and postcards. Look out for DK currency notes, printed in China but never introduced into circulation, as the Khmer Rouge decided to ban not just markets, but currency as well. The notes, which feature guerrilla fighters and happy, productive peasants, are therefore in excellent condition.

You may want to take a taxi to go back to central Phnom Penh.

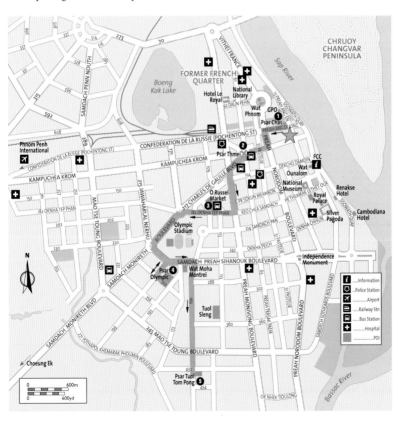

Wat Phnom

According to Cambodian legend, around six centuries ago a woman by the name of Penh found some Buddha figures by the bank of the Sap River. Being both rich and pious, she had a temple constructed to house them on top of a nearby hill. In fact the hill was little more than a mound, but for all that, the highest natural point in the vicinity. Hence the area was named Phnom Penh or 'Hill of Penh'.

Wat Phnom, the temple built to house the figures, is entered from the east via a short stairway with *naga* balustrades. The main *vihara*, or temple sanctuary, has been rebuilt several times, most recently in 1926. The walls are painted with murals from the *Reamker* – the Khmer version of the Indian *Ramayana* – and a small pavilion to the south houses a statue of Penh, the temple's founder. Although dedicated to Theravada Buddhism, it is also home to a shrine for Preah Chau, a deity especially revered by the city's Vietnamese community, whilst on the table in front are representations of Confucius and two Daoist sages. Finally to the left of the central altar is an eight-armed statue of the Hindu deity Vishnu.

Wat Phnom, Phnom Penh

The large *chedi* to the west of the temple sanctuary holds the ashes of King Ponhea Yat (1405–67). Those who wish may take a short elephant ride around the mound on which the temple sits.
Street 96 and Norodom Boulevard.
Open: daily 6am–6pm.
Admission charge.

Wat Preah Keo (Silver Pagoda)

The celebrated Silver Pagoda is considered to house the palladium of the nation, and photography within the building is forbidden. It was built by King Norodom in 1892, and extensively rebuilt by King Sihanouk in 1962. It houses two priceless Buddha figures, one of which – the Emerald Buddha, from which the temple gets its name – dates from the 17th century and is made of crystal. The other is a much larger affair, being made of 90kg (198lb) of pure gold, encrusted with 9,584 diamonds, the largest of which is 25 carats.

There are clear similarities between Phnom Penh's Silver Pagoda and Wat Phra Kaeo in Bangkok, and this is particularly true of the pagoda courtyard which is painted with a 640m (2,100ft) long series of murals from the Hindu *Ramayana* or *Reamker*, featuring Rama's struggle to free his kidnapped paramour Sita from Ravana, the evil demon-king of Lanka. Rama is helped in this epic fight by the monkey-king Hanuman, and his army of monkeys. The murals were painted in 1903, very

Part of the Silver Pagoda, Royal Palace, Phnom Penh

much after the style of the similar murals in Bangkok. Although partially protected from the elements by a covered cloister, they have suffered badly from rain damage and water seepage and are in need of urgent restoration. They should be viewed clockwise, starting with the gallery showing the birth of Lord Rama.
Exit the main Royal Palace compound in the southeast corner and enter the north gate of the Silver Pagoda, Samdech Sothearos Boulevard. Open: daily 7.30–11am & 2–5pm. Admission included in Royal Palace entrance ticket.

North of Phnom Penh

The area to the immediate north of Phnom Penh, lying between the capital and the country's third largest city, Kompong Cham, is a fascinating region encompassing royal tombs, rubber plantations, an important Hindu temple and a broad stretch of the great Mekong River, not to mention some unusual and not necessarily appealing culinary possibilities.

Kompong Cham is a principal river port with a population of 65,000, the capital of a lush province of the same name that traditionally makes a living by fishing, rice farming and extensive rubber plantations. Its Khmer name means 'Cham Village', but in fact most people living here are ethnic Khmers, while the Cham Muslims (*see pp46–7*) constitute a small but colourful minority community. A new bridge, built with Japanese funding, links the city with the east bank of the Mekong and the nearby Vietnamese province of Tay Ninh.

Attractions in the province include a number of pre-Angkor Period and Angkor Period temples, as well as boating and fishing by the banks of the mighty Mekong River. Two former royal capitals, Udong and Lovek, stand on the left bank of the Sap River and are worth visiting. Further afield, the river ports of Kratie and Stung Treng have some fine old colonial architecture, while a small group of endangered Irrawaddy dolphins live in the water not far from Kratie.

Kompong Cham

Kompong Cham is Cambodia's third largest city and an important communications hub, but it remains a quiet enough place, the more so since the new Japanese Bridge across the Mekong River has made the constant back-and-forth traffic of ferries across the river no longer necessary. This may change in the near future, however, as the provincial authorities in the nearby Vietnamese province of Tay Ninh have announced plans to upgrade the road between Tay Ninh and Kompong Cham, creating a major new highway between Ho Chi Minh City (Saigon) and Phnom Penh.

There are no major attractions in the city itself, though there are some attractive old buildings, and the **Mekong Hotel**, located right on the waterfront, provides a pleasant location to have a drink or something to eat

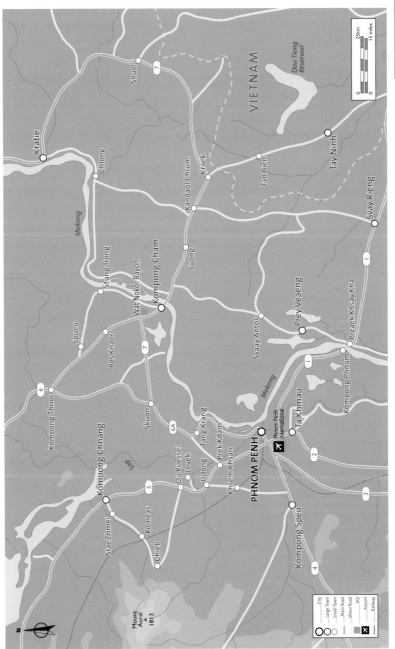

A French colonial building, now a police station, Kompong Cham

whilst watching life on the great river which sweeps endlessly by. Small boats with one or two fishermen cast their nets and drift slowly downstream. Occasional ferryboats still ply the river, and quite large cargo ships chug upstream against the muddy waters, ready to take on or offload cargo. Much of Cambodia's considerable rubber exports exits the country this way, sailing all the way down through Vietnam to the South China Sea.

It seems unlikely today, but during the French period Kompong Cham was a major rubber transhipment point, with significant numbers of colonial planters making a good living in the rubber and tobacco businesses. Though these Western residents are long since gone, the wide, tree-lined streets laid out in a grid pattern, and the numerous,

rather rundown French-style colonial houses are a mute testimony to this past.

Just outside of town – about 2km (1¼ miles) to the northwest – the 8th-century temple of **Wat Nokor Bayon** is worth visiting. Originally a Mahayana Buddhist shrine, it was rededicated to Theravada Buddhism, Cambodia's major religious tradition, at some point in the 15th century. The venerable sandstone and laterite structures of the ancient temple blend well with an active modern temple, ochre-robed monks and the sound of chanting, creating a fascinating mix of the contemporary and the archaic. There are several ancient Buddha images, and one large, more modern reclining Buddha.

Just to the south of town the river island of **Koh Pbain** is a popular picnic spot for locals. In the dry season it can be reached by a rickety bamboo bridge that is taken down and reassembled on an annual basis as the waters rise. The inhabitants are mainly Cham Muslims (*see pp46–7*) whose men fish the river while the women weave silk and cotton *kramaa* on looms set up in the shade beneath their stilt houses.

National Highway 7, 120km (75 miles) northeast of Phnom Penh. Air-con buses take two hours and leave Phnom Penh every hour during the day.

Lovek

Lovek is another former royal city. Situated on the west bank of the Sap River, it was the Cambodian capital between the times of Angkor and Udong, and flourished for a short period during the 16th century. In 1594, the city was captured and looted by the expanding Siamese Kingdom of Ayutthaya. Local histories record that forces from Ayutthaya attacked the city in 1593, but without success. Before leaving, however, the wily Siamese fired silver coins by cannon into the bamboo fortifications surrounding the Lovek. After their withdrawal, the Cambodians dismantled these barricades to get at the silver. As a consequence, when the Siamese returned a year later, they were able to capture the city with ease. Today little remains of the former Cambodian capital beyond the ramparts and moats in a very rural setting. There is a small shrine at the entrance with two statues representing the Khmer general who defeated the Thai forces attacking Lovek in 1593.

About 5km (3 miles) east of Udong.

Cows and paddy fields on the Kompong Cham Loop

The Cham

The Cham are perhaps the oldest and least-known people of Indochina. Inheritors of a proud tradition that stretches back almost two millennia, Champa was the first Indianised kingdom in Indochina. Its founding predates both the beginnings of Cambodia in about AD 550 and the first major expansion of the Vietnamese south from the Red River Delta in the mid-10th century.

At the peak of their power, about 12 centuries ago, the Cham controlled rich and fertile lands stretching from north of Hue, in central Annam, to the Mekong Delta in Cochinchina. But with the emergence of the powerful Cambodian Kingdom of Angkor in about AD 800, and the renewal of Vietnam's territorial expansion to the south just over a century later, Champa found itself hopelessly outnumbered and caught in a vice between Cambodia and Vietnam. This vice gradually tightened with the Vietnamese, in particular, pushing the Cham south towards the Mekong Delta.

In 1471 the outnumbered Cham suffered a massive defeat at the hands of the Vietnamese. Some 60,000 of their soldiers were reportedly killed, and another 60,000 taken into captivity. Champa was reduced to a small sliver of territory in the region of Nha Trang, which survived until 1720, when the king and many of his subjects fled to neighbouring Cambodia rather than submit to Vietnamese conquest. The Cham Diaspora dates from this period, and the diverse Cham communities later established in Cambodia can trace their origin to this catastrophe.

Most Cham refugees moved further up the Mekong, into territories that now constitute the Cambodian heartland. They settled along the

Cham Muslims (historical image)

Vendor and her plate of tasty fried tarantulas, Skuon

faith of their ancestors, caught fish, grew rice, and tried to stay out of the way, being by and large neutral in the war that was destroying Cambodia.

Yet during the three and a half years of Khmer Rouge rule Cambodia's Cham were systematically victimised. All mosques – traditionally the spiritual and social centres of Cham community life – were either demolished, or given over for use as ammunition stores, military barracks and even pigsties. By the time the Khmer Rouge regime was toppled in December 1978, between one half and two thirds of the Cham had been murdered, starved to death or driven to flee the country. Today the community is slowly recovering from this trauma.

banks of the great river north and east of Phnom Penh, notably in the appropriately named province and town of Kompong Cham, but also along the shores of Tonlé Sap, Cambodia's fertile inland lake. Here they became well known and relatively prosperous through their skills as fishermen, settling into the ebb and flow of Cambodian life, and acquiring a widespread reputation for their abilities as fisherfolk and practitioners of traditional medicine.

In 1975, when the Khmer Rouge seized power in Cambodia, nearly 400,000 Cham were living as peaceably as times permitted in just over two hundred towns and villages along the Mekong north and east of Phnom Penh. They followed the Islamic

A TASTE FOR TARANTULA

Skuon is known throughout Cambodia for a popular local delicacy – tarantula. These large, hairy, poisonous spiders live in burrows in the surrounding area, and are assiduously dug up by hand by the locals. They are either deep fried and served on plates to passing drivers at busy Skuon markets, or bottled in white liquor and served as 'tarantula wine' for their supposed potency as an aphrodisiac. In some recent Western accounts of this custom, it has been suggested that the people of Skuon took to eating (and selling) tarantulas during the starvation years of the Khmer Rouge regime. Not a bit of it! Tarantulas are highly esteemed as a tasty foodstuff, and don't come cheap by local standards.

Vendors next to the Mekong River, near Kratie

The Mekong upstream

Beyond Kompong Cham the Mekong winds north and then sharply east for around 100km (62 miles), or about three hours' journey by fast boat, to the provincial capital of **Kratie**. There is a dilapidated charm to this isolated riverside port which still retains some fine, if mouldering, examples of French colonial architecture. There are several passable hotels along the waterfront by the dock, and a few restaurants serving chiefly Cambodian and Chinese dishes. The waterfront also has a number of bars and cafés selling beer and soft drinks, and these make a good spot to sit and watch the sunset over the Mekong. The riverfront is also the place to charter a boat a short distance down river to experience Kratie's main attraction – Irrawaddy dolphin watching (*see box opposite*).

From Kratie it is possible to charter a boat or take a taxi 30km (19 miles) north of town to the peaceful riverside village of **Sambor**. In the vicinity are pre-Angkor ruins dating from the 7th–8th centuries, but pending excavation and restoration there is relatively little to see. Beyond Kratie the Mekong continues north for 140km (87 miles) to the isolated riverside town of **Stung Treng**. Highway 13 from Kratie to Stung Treng runs inland, some distance from the river, whilst the latter attains widths of several kilometres in these remote reaches. It takes between three and four hours to reach Stung Treng by fast boat from Kratie.

The town of Stung Treng stands on the banks of the San River a short distance from the Mekong. It's a small place, surprisingly clean, with a well-maintained park beside the riverfront. Passable accommodation is available, and the usual selection of Khmer and Chinese dishes is served in a few small restaurants located to the west of the town market. There's not much to see in this sleepy backwater, but Stung Treng does make a suitable base for trips up river and a last reasonably comfortable stopover for those taking the long road east through the wilds of Ratanakiri Province, home to some of Cambodia's most remote tribal peoples. It's also possible to cross the Mekong by boat from Stung Treng to the small settlement of Phumi Thalabarivat where the ruins of a brick-built pre-Angkor temple may be visited.

Udong

The former royal capital of Udong, meaning 'victorious' in Khmer, is located on low hills to the west of the Sap River and north of Phnom Penh. It was the capital of Cambodia on several

Primitive-looking Buddha figure at the post-Angkorean capital of Udong

IRRAWADDY DOLPHINS

During recent decades these delightful and sociable mammals were driven to the verge of extinction by fishing with explosives and nets, as well as fatal encounters with propellers. Today, however, tourism seems to be providing an economic stimulus for their protection. The boatmen of Kratie say they never kill dolphins intentionally, but they certainly know where they are to be found and will take visitors to see them for around US$5 an hour. One such destination is the village of Prek Kampi about 17km (11 miles) south of Kratie, where a pod of around 20 dolphins live. They are said to appear regularly every morning and evening, but the locals claim the best time to see them is around three in the afternoon.

occasions between the abandonment of Angkor in 1618 and the move to Phnom Penh in 1866. Today little remains of the former capital's days of glory, but the area is still well worth a visit. Two small hills rise from the surrounding plains, though both were badly deforested by bombing during the war years, and many of the former royal stupas have been destroyed or are in ruins. The larger of the two hills is called Phnom Reach Throap, or 'Hill of the Royal Treasury'. Here visitors can see the remains of a great Buddha image blown up by the Khmer Rouge, and stupas containing the ashes of Udong's 17th-century founder, King Soriyopor, as well as King Ang Duong (1845–60) and King Monivong (1927–41).

35km (22 miles) north of Phnom Penh just off National Highway 5. A hired taxi or bus takes one hour.

Drive: The Kompong Cham Loop

Udong, a former royal capital of Cambodia, can be visited from Phnom Penh on a day trip. If time permits, a more rewarding and informative trip may be made by driving to stay overnight at the river port city of Kompong Cham, with the option of returning by boat to Phnom Penh the next day.

Allow two days for this drive or combined drive and voyage, which covers about 250km (155 miles).

Drive northwest out of Phnom Penh across the Chruoy Changvar Bridge and continue past small Cham Muslim settlements (see pp46–7) along Highway 5 to Prek Kdam. Continue past the ferry for a further 8km (5 miles) to Udong.

1 Udong

Udong was badly damaged by USAF B-52 bombers during the Second Indochina War, and subsequently depopulated by the Khmer Rouge. It's worth visiting, however, for attractive Wat Udong and for views of the surrounding countryside. (*See also p49.*)
To reach Lovek, go north from Udong for about 3km (2 miles) then go right for another 2km (1¼ miles) past an old military college.

2 Lovek

(*See p45.*)
Backtrack from Lovek to Prek Kdam and take the car ferry across the Sap River. Follow National Highway 6 northeast for about 45km (28 miles) to Skuon.

3 Skuon

The market town of Skuon is a good place to stop for a bite to eat, but watch what you buy, as Skuon is known locally as 'Spiderville' and is celebrated for its tarantula snacks.
Continue east from Skuon along Highway 7 for 45km (28 miles). Kompong Cham is really the only place to stay overnight on this drive.

4 Kompong Cham

(*See pp42–5.*)

5 The Mekong River

Abandon your land transport and catch the single daily express boat from Kratie to Phnom Penh, a fascinating journey down the Mekong. Taking about two hours from Kompong Cham, the boat moors north of Sisowath Quay in Phnom Penh.
The Kratie–Phnom Penh express boat stops by the Mekong Hotel between 9.30 and 10am daily.

Drive: The Kompong Cham Loop

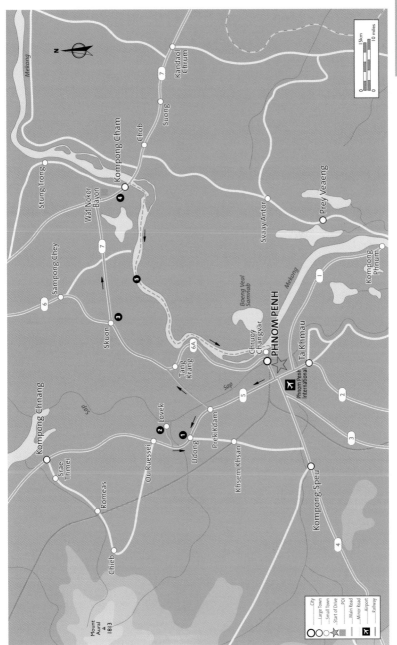

Preah Vihear

Perched on a 600m (1,970ft) cliff on the edge of the Dangrek Mountains high above the Cambodian plains, Preah Vihear was founded by King Rajendravarman II in the mid-10th century and completed by King Surayavarman II in the 12th century. Built in the Baphuon and early Angkor styles, it was designed as a Hindu temple and dedicated to the god Shiva.

The temple is built on a north–south axis, and consists essentially of a causeway and steps leading up a steep hill to the main sanctuary, located precariously on the edge of the Dangrek escarpment. The approach to the sanctuary is punctuated by five *gopura* (elaborate gateways). Each *gopura* opens onto a courtyard and is reached by a flight of steps, increasing the dramatic impact of the ascent. The *gopura* impede the view of successive parts of the temple, making it impossible to see the complex as a whole from any one point and adding to the numinous impact of the setting.

A group of monks and novices, Preah Vihear

Two of the main *gopura* have collapsed, but details of finely carved *apsara* (celestial dancing girls) remain visible. The third *gopura* is comparatively well preserved, with a beautiful lintel depicting Shiva and his consort Uma seated on Nandi, the bull. The temple extends for around 800m (2,625ft) through five separate stages, before culminating in the massive bulk of the main sanctuary. Here the great *prasat* or central spire has fallen to the ground and great blocks of carved stone lie in piles, a giant's jigsaw puzzle awaiting eventual restoration. Everywhere there are signs warning visitors not to stray off the sanctioned paths, for the danger of mines remains very real. On a clear day the dizzying views from the cliff top are truly spectacular.

A geographical peculiarity of Preah Vihear is its location. Nobody doubts that it was built by Cambodians and that it is culturally Khmer, but shifting frontiers over the centuries mean that the temple is all but inaccessible from modern Cambodia, while it is easily accessed from neighbouring Thailand. Long claimed by both countries, the complex was eventually awarded to Cambodia by the World Court in 1963, a decision that still rankles with many Thais. Closed to visitors for decades, the temple opened again from the Thai side at the end of 1998.

Monks at Preah Vihear

Cambodia completed the construction of a basic access road up the cliff in 2003, but it remains much easier to visit as a day trip from Thailand.

Possible bases for a visit to Preah Vihear are the Thai cities of Surin, Sisaket and Ubon Ratchathani. All have good accommodation and restaurants, though only Surin and Ubon have first-class hotels. An alternative is to stay in the small town of Kantharalak, just 30km (19 miles) north of Preah Vihear. The temple is best visited as a day trip. Cambodia allows day-trip access to the temple on a visa-free basis from Thailand. *Cambodia imposes an entrance charge, plus a separate fee for processing a copy of the passport. In addition, Thailand imposes an access fee for entering the Khao Phra Wihan National Park.*

South of Phnom Penh

Takeo Province, which borders Vietnam, is a worthwhile destination offering the busy visitor a chance to see some fine examples of Khmer temple architecture without going to Angkor. Because of its proximity to Phnom Penh, it is possible to visit some of these temples on a day trip from the capital. An interesting alternative is to stay overnight in the provincial capital, also called Takeo, visiting the various temples at leisure.

The province is traditionally part of Cambodia's 'rice bowl', an area of rich paddy fields and sugar palms that have supplied Phnom Penh with food for generations. The area is also roughly commensurate with 'Water Chen La' (*see pp62–3*), the earliest known Cambodian civilisation dating from the 5th–6th centuries, before the Khmer capital was moved to the Angkor region. Today the remains of 'Water Chen La' can be visited at Angkor Borei and Phnom Da to the east of Takeo.

Closer to Phnom Penh, the 12th-century shrines of Ta Prohm and Yeah Peau are the best-preserved Khmer temples in the vicinity of the capital and make an ideal picnic location. The impressive temple of Phnom Chisor stands atop the hill after which it was named and offers magnificent views across the countryside.

Angkor Borei

Archaeologists believe that, some 1,200 years ago, the small southern market town of Angkor Borei was the location of Vyadhapura, part of 'Water Chen La', the first Cambodian kingdom before the Khmer capital moved to Angkor. Until recently there was little concrete evidence for this, but since 1996, in a continuing investigation, archaeologists from the University of Hawaii, working with local Cambodian colleagues, have uncovered ancient walls and irrigation channels, as well as several collapsed brick structures, stone stele and ceramic pots. The centre for these investigations is a low on which a more modern temple, Wat Komnou, currently stands. The visitor should check out Angkor Borei District Office (*open: daily 8.30am–noon, 2–4.30pm. Admission charge*), a lovely old colonial-style building, where some Chen La relics are displayed including a Shiva *lingam*, early inscriptions and temple carvings. *20km (12½ miles) east of Takeo. A hired boat from Takeo takes 35 minutes. In the dry season it is possible to take a taxi for the visit.*

Phnom Chisor

The Buddhist temple complex of Phnom Chisor stands atop Chisor Mountain to the east of National Highway 2. The turnoff is indicated by the two brick towers of Prasat Neang Khmau, the 'Temple of the Black Virgin', once dedicated to the Hindu goddess Kali. It's a long and tiring climb to the top of the hill, involving as many as 750 unevenly spaced concrete steps, but the effort is worth it because of the spectacular views over the surrounding countryside. Snacks and cold drinks are available on the way up and at the top, and you should make at least two rest stops to take advantage of the wonderful views.

The main temple stands on the eastern side of the hill. Constructed of brick and laterite with lintels and doorways of sandstone, the complex dates from the 11th century when it was known as Suryagiri. The isolation of the site, and the way the temple suddenly appears as the visitor crests the hill, has led some to liken Phnom Chisor's atmosphere to that of a

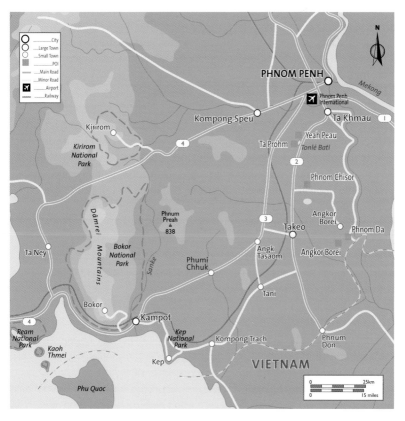

Southeast Asian Machu Picchu. Views from the far side of the temple, looking due east, are truly impressive. The long, straight road built by the original temple architects is clearly discernible, and would make a far more suitable entry point if reclaimed from the encroaching jungle. Two smaller temples punctuate the progress of this road, and a big natural lake can be seen on the horizon.

52km (32 miles) south of Phnom Penh turn off National Highway 2 to the east and continue for 4km (2½ miles). A taxi takes about 1½ hours. Open: daily 8.30am–5.30pm. Admission charge.

Phnom Da

This hilltop temple, which dates back to the 7th or 8th century, is built of brick and sandstone. Despite being one of the oldest stone buildings in Cambodia, it is in an unexpectedly good state of preservation. Close by on another hilly protrusion is a smaller sandstone temple, believed to have been constructed about a century after Phnom Da, called Asram Taa Asey. This structure is thought to have been dedicated to Harihara, a god combining manifestations of Vishnu and Shiva in the same deity.

The area around Angkor Borei is very low-lying and liable to flooding in the rainy season. While it's possible to drive to the temples in the dry season, it may be necessary to take a small boat from Angkor Borei during the rains.

About 5km (3 miles) from Angkor Borei. Continue in the hired boat for 15 minutes. Open: daily 8.30am–5.30pm. Admission charge.

Ta Prohm

The small settlement of Tonlé Bati is a popular weekend destination for citizens of the Cambodian capital, who go there to fish and picnic beside Lake Bati, as well as to see the ancient temples in the locality.

The chief attraction at Tonlé Bati is the laterite temple of Ta Prohm, built by King Jayavarman VII on top of an earlier 6th-century Khmer shrine. Ta Prohm is a well-preserved gem of a temple, not unduly large, but with some splendid decorative features. The main sanctuary has five chambers, in each of which is a statue or a Shiva *lingam*. At times the shrine is favoured by fortune-tellers who will predict the future and read palms for a few Cambodian riel. It's also quite common to find Khmer music being played at the temple, either by a few monks or – especially at weekends – by a traditional Cambodian orchestra.

One special feature of the temple can be found on the east wall of the sanctuary, about 3.5m (11½ft) above the ground. This is a bas-relief showing a woman carrying a box on her head whilst a man bows in apparent supplication to another, larger woman. According to tradition, the story represented is that of a pregnant woman who gave birth with the help of a midwife, to whom she then failed to show sufficient respect. As a punishment, the midwife condemned her to carry the afterbirth in a box on her head for the rest of her life. The man is begging the midwife to forgive his wife. Another unusual bas-relief on (*cont. on p60*)

Stone pediment, Phnom Chisor temple

Oc Eo and Funan

Experts tend to disagree over the origins of the Cambodian people, some suggesting that they originated from the south, in present-day Malaysia and Indonesia, whilst others believe they may have migrated from further north, in the region of southern China. What is clear is that the fertile floodplains of the lower Mekong, as well as the Tonlé Sap Lake, were inhabited by people who were the ancestors of today's Cambodians at least 4,000 years ago.

Little is known about these ancient people. They baked earthenware pots to hold water and fermented toddy palm, or to store the plentiful fish in which the region has always abounded. It was a forested region, with plenty of wood, which also flooded frequently.

Conditions for sedentary agriculture were unusually rich. The waters teemed with fish, rice could be grown with a relative modicum of effort, and simple boats were built to travel from stilt house to stilt house, and village to village. The region, moreover, was close to the South China Sea, with easy access to the developing trade

Ta Prohm sits on an important 6th-century Funan era site

Central shrine, Ta Prohm, built over a
6th-century Funan era shrine

the maritime trade between India, Southeast Asia and China. The territory once owned by Funan in the fertile Mekong Delta was eventually occupied by Vietnam in the 18th and 19th centuries. Besides the ruins of Oc Eo, near Rach Gia in the southern Mekong Delta, a series of ceramic pots, beads and similar artefacts preserved in museums at Hanoi, Saigon and Long Xuyen is all that is left of Funan's material culture.

Funan may have gone into decline with the Arabs' discovery of the monsoon winds, which permitted direct transoceanic travel, as opposed to coastal navigation. On the other hand, this vital development, which occurred some time in the early centuries AD, might equally well have led to a growth in the commerce and economic prosperity of Funan.

By about AD 500 Funan appears to have been in general decline, whilst a new polity was developing further inland, near the confluence of the Mekong and Sap Rivers, in the region of present-day Phnom Penh. The inhabitants of this state, known to the Chinese annals (and therefore to subsequent history) as Chen La, spoke a Mon-Khmer language, were strongly influenced by Indian religious traditions, and may be regarded as the progenitors of the first authentically Cambodian state.

routes between China, Southeast Asia and the Middle East. In short, all the prerequisites existed for the development of a potentially rich and advanced civilisation – which, from around the 1st century AD, was exactly what happened.

The first civilisation to appear in the Cambodian region was the Kingdom of Funan, almost nothing of which survives today beyond the ruins of the supposed capital, Oc Eo, deep in the south Vietnamese delta province of An Giang. Oc Eo was a trading port which flourished, researchers believe, between about AD 100 and 500, after which it became submerged, not to be rediscovered until the 1940s. A precursor to the great Khmer Empire that flourished between the 9th and 15th centuries, Funan prospered on the inner north wall of the central sanctuary shows a king sitting with his consort. Because she has been unfaithful, a servant is represented in the lower part of the carving putting her to death by trampling her with a horse.

31km (19 miles) south of Phnom Penh turn off National Highway 2 to the west and proceed for 2.5km (1½ miles). A taxi takes about an hour. Open: daily 8.30am–5.30pm. Admission charge.

Takeo

Takeo is a sleepy country town that makes an agreeable place to stop for the night. The hotels are satisfactory, and both Khmer and Chinese food is readily obtainable. One would hardly guess that, during the Khmer Rouge period, Takeo was the headquarters of Ta Mok, the much-feared one-legged general who died in prison in 2006 while awaiting trial for genocide and crimes against humanity (*see box*). 'Grandfather Mok' and his soldiers made Takeo the most feared region in Cambodia, though happily there is little sign of those days now. There won't be a lot happening in Takeo – visitors should eat, have a few quiet drinks, and retire early with a view to an equally early morning start.

77km (48 miles) south of Phnom Penh on National Highway 2. A share taxi or bus takes two hours.

Yeah Peau

Just to the north of Ta Prohm stands the second of Tonlé Bati's attractions, the small but exquisite temple of Yeah Peau. According to legend, during the 12th century King Preah Ket Mealea was travelling in the Tonlé Bati area when he met and fell in love with a young girl called Peau. Soon Peau became pregnant, and after a while gave birth to a boy whom she named Prohm. The king in the meantime had returned to Angkor, leaving Peau with a ring and a sacred dagger so that the boy could journey to Angkor and identify himself to the king when he had come of age. Eventually this came to pass, and Prohm travelled to Angkor where he lived with his father for several years.

TA MOK

The elusive, one-legged Khmer Rouge commander, Chhit Chhoeun – better known by the *nom-de-guerre* of Ta Mok, or 'Grandfather Mok' – was Pol Pot's most trusted military lieutenant. Born in Takeo in 1926, he became a Buddhist monk as a youth, but later joined the anti-French resistance and, subsequently, the Cambodian Communist Party. By the late 1960s he was a general and the group's chief-of-staff. He was also a member of the Standing Committee of the Khmer Rouge's Central Committee during its period in power. He became very influential within the party, especially in the Southwest Zone centred on Takeo. Mok is believed to have directed many of the purges that characterised Khmer Rouge rule, earning him the nickname 'butcher'. After the fall of the DK regime he fought on as a guerrilla leader, eventually deposing and arresting Pol Pot in 1997. In 1999 Mok was himself arrested, dying in captivity in Phnom Penh on 21 July 2006, before he could be brought to trial.

In time Prohm returned to Tonlé Bati, but failed to recognise his mother, seeing instead a woman so attractive that he fell in love with her and asked her to become his wife. Peau recognised her son, and told him that she was his mother, but the young man refused to believe it. Accordingly, it was decided that a temple-building contest should be held to determine what should be done. If Prohm, assisted by the local men, could build a temple before Peau, assisted by the local women, then she would marry him. In the event the wily Peau created the illusion of a rising morning star by lighting a candle. The men, thinking it was already dawn and that the women could not possibly beat them, went to sleep. The women, however, continued building and went on to win the contest. In this way Prohm was obliged to acknowledge Peau as his mother.

That, at least, is the local legend. Whatever the real facts behind the building of Tonlé Bati, two exquisite temples exist, one – Ta Prohm – named for the son, and the other – Yeah Peau – named for his mother. Inside the latter, which is the smaller of the two temples, there is a statue of Peau venerating a seated Buddha.

150m (165yd) to the north of Ta Prohm. Open: daily 8.30am–5.30pm. Admission included with ticket to Ta Prohm.

Sunrise over 'Water Chen La', near Takeo

From 'Water Chen La' to 'Land Chen La'

By around AD 800 the Khmer state referred to as 'Chen La' in the Chinese annals had developed into a Cambodian kingdom with its capital at Isanapura – now known as Sambor Prei Kuk, near Kompong Thom. At the time, Isanapura is said to have been the largest existing complex of stone structures anywhere in mainland Southeast Asia.

The view across 'Water Chen La' from Phnom Chisor temple

Regrettably, few records exist which can give a precise picture of Cambodian society – let alone life for the average Cambodian – in this distant past. The sources we have available are limited to Sanskrit and Khmer stone inscriptions, and to the records compiled by the Chinese. Fortunately, for several centuries and certainly from the 3rd century AD, tributary missions were sent from the region to China, and Chinese traders and adventurers similarly travelled in the other direction.

One early Chinese description recounts that: 'The king's dwelling had a double terrace on it. Palisades take the place of walls in fortified places… The king rides mounted on an elephant. His subjects are of ill-favoured appearance and black; their hair is frizzy; they wear neither clothing nor shoes. For a living, they cultivate the soil; they sow one year, and reap for three… These barbarians are not without their own history books; they even have archives for their texts.'

Yet such evocative accounts are sadly rare, offering little more than a small window into the distant Khmer past. Around the mid-6th century, moreover, tributary missions appear to have stopped, perhaps at about the same time as Chen La began its rise to eclipse the earlier kingdoms of Oc Eo and Funan. Certainly little enough is known of Chen La, or of why and how it developed.

Modern scholarship tends to believe that Chen La was a loose confederation of small Khmer-speaking kingdoms rather than, as was once thought, a powerful centralised state. It is interesting to note that contemporaneous Chinese sources distinguish between 'Water Chen La' (which may have been in the Mekong Delta) and 'Land Chen La' which, as the name suggests, lay further inland.

By around 800 'Land Chen La' seems to have eclipsed 'Water Chen La' in power and importance, as the centre of the Cambodian polity moved northwards and westwards, beyond Isanapura, and towards the region which would eventually become Angkor. At the same time the state seems to have gained a new solidity, though precisely why remains uncertain. The eminent historian of Cambodia David Chandler suggests that this development involved increasing population density, improved wet-rice farming techniques, and victories in local,

A typical southern 'Water Chen La' Cambodian agricultural scene

unrecorded wars, with the latter perhaps resulting in an extended period of peace.

By around 850 'Land Chen La' was developing into an increasingly rich and centralised kingdom. Furthermore, as the Cambodian centre moved further inland, away from the coast, it relied less on subsistence agriculture and trade, more on manpower, irrigation technology and concentrated rice production. In this way the foundations were steadily laid for the establishment of the great Khmer Empire which would develop in the region of Roluos and Angkor.

The coast

The Cambodian coast, once celebrated as the 'Cambodian Riviera', was a palm-fringed playground for the Cambodian elite before the outbreak of the Second Indochina War. During the war years all this changed, as the area was devastated and, subsequently, largely depopulated by the Khmer Rouge. Today it has recovered and is once again an idyll of unspoiled tree-lined beaches, warm tropical waters and – increasingly – good hotels.

There's no shortage of things to do in the coastal area. On the coast itself there are facilities for deep-sea fishing and scuba diving offshore wrecks, while closer to shore there are good locations for fishing and snorkelling, water-skiing, wind surfing and plain old swimming and sunbathing. Fresh seafood is plentiful and of excellent quality. The area isn't yet too touristy, but if you want to get away from the 'crowd' on the beaches, there are plenty of pristine islands to visit where you can often be quite on your own.

Inland but within easy striking distance of the coast there are national parks at Kirirom and Bokor, both offering fine hiking opportunities amid pine-covered hills. Ream National Park extends over a protected marine area, as well as unspoiled hill country. Sihanoukville, the area's main city and Cambodia's only deep-water port, has four beach areas, numerous restaurants, bars and cafés, and the nation's best nightlife after Phnom Penh. Finally, Sre Ambel at the foot of the Dâmrei and Cardamom Mountains is a gateway to unspoiled wilderness and opportunities for 'extreme hiking', with guides, for the adventurous and seriously fit.

THE CAMBODIAN RIVIERA

In times past, the Cambodian coast enjoyed an idyllic reputation amongst middle class Cambodians, French colonialists and wealthy foreign visitors alike. Perhaps because of this association with domestic and foreign elites, the palm-fringed southern coast – a region studded with the elaborate villas of the wealthy – fared particularly badly under the harsh rule of the Khmer Rouge. Kep was razed to the ground, whilst ordinary people – except a few fishermen – were moved away from the coast to prevent the possibility of flight by sea. Even the movements of those permitted to fish were tightly monitored by Khmer Rouge cadres, whilst traffic through the port of Kompong Som was limited to the exchange of Cambodian raw materials for Chinese and North Korean arms. Fortunately, the situation has changed dramatically, and today the 'Cambodian Riviera' is making a comeback.

Bokor

Renowned in pre-war days for its pleasant climate, cool mountain streams, forested walks and distant panoramic view of the Gulf of Thailand, Bokor fell on hard times under the Khmer Rouge and is still mainly in ruins. It's worth a visit for the idyllic mountain views and the somewhat eerie atmosphere – and as recently as 2007, the authorities announced plans to rebuild the resort. The 1,079m (3,540ft) high resort is often shrouded in mist, which drifts through the ruins of the once magnificent Bokor Palace Hotel, King Sihanouk's abandoned Black Palace residence, and the shell of an old colonial church. A popular trek is to Popokvil Waterfall, in fact twin falls 15m and 18m (49ft and 59ft) high, situated a 40-minute walk beyond the ruined resort. All Bokor's sights lie within the Bokor National Park.
41km (26 miles) northwest of Kampot and 190km (118 miles) southwest of Phnom Penh. National Park open daily. Admission charge.

Kampot

Kampot shelters in the lee of the Dâmrei or Elephant Mountains, a wild region of trackless forests and sheer, unclimbed rock outcrops. The town centres on a rather drab roundabout where the main hotels are located.

The coast

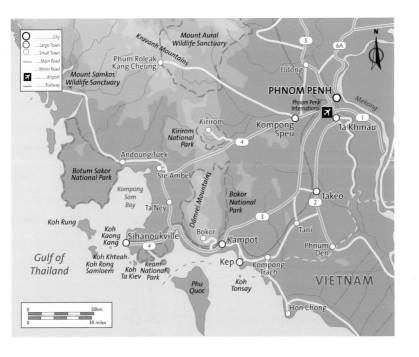

The view towards the Dâmrei Mountains across Prek Kompong Bay, Kampot

To the north is a busy covered market popular with visitors from Phnom Penh seeking fresh seafood. More interesting to the visitor are the narrow, colonnaded streets leading west from the roundabout to the riverfront. Although badly in need of restoration, there are some fine examples of French and Chinese colonial architecture to be seen in this area, as well as the best of Kampot's handful of restaurants.

Travellers staying overnight in Kampot should check into one of the hotels at the roundabout, head east towards the river for a bite to eat, then walk the length of the delightful riverfront which, shaded by casuarina trees, offers fine views of the nearby Dâmrei Mountains. There are some

particularly fine colonial buildings in this area, notably the Governor's Residence and the main post office at the southern end of the riverfront. *148km (92 miles) southwest of Phnom Penh on National Highway 3. A share taxi or bus takes two hours.*

Kep

In pre-war times this beautiful stretch of tree-lined beach was home to the villas of rich Cambodians and French settlers. Then the Khmer Rouge arrived and destroyed virtually every building in town, turning the Shell petrol station into a mass grave. Today Kep is back on the tourist circuit, though much rebuilding remains to be done. A short distance off the Kep shore lies **Koh**

Tonsay, also known as 'Rabbit Island', which can easily be reached by boat and makes a popular excursion. The island has four small but beautiful beaches with good swimming and snorkelling. The large island clearly visible to the south is Phu Quoc and belongs to Vietnam, though Cambodia disputes this status. *25km (16 miles) southeast of Kampot. Rent a share taxi or moto in Kampot.*

Sihanoukville

The port and resort city of Sihanoukville, also known as Kompong Som, boasts about 10km (6 miles) of beachfront, divided into four main beaches. Starting in the north, the first of these is Victory Beach between the

THE MAYAGÜEZ INCIDENT

The Mayagüez Incident marked the last official battle of the United States in the Second Indochina War. On 12 May 1975, 12 days after the fall of Saigon to the North Vietnamese Army, Khmer Rouge speedboats seized the American container ship SS *Mayagüez* in international waters off Sihanoukville. Denouncing the action as piracy, US President Ford sent the aircraft carrier USS *Coral Sea* into the area, as well as transferring a substantial force of marines from Subic Bay to U-Tapao Air Force Base in nearby Thailand. In the action that followed 41 US servicemen lost their lives, as well as an estimated 60 Khmer Rouge. Ironically, the crew of the *Mayagüez* had already been released, unbeknown to the US authorities, before the rescue mission was launched.

The coast

Old French colonial mansion, Kep

harbour and Koh Pos Island – really two beaches divided by a rocky point and a small hillock. About 2km (1¼ miles) long, the northern end is more developed, with several restaurants and budget-priced bungalows. Independence Beach, between the site of the old Independence Hotel and the southwestern peninsula, is popular with weekenders in from the capital but is often deserted mid-week. Sokha Beach, between the peninsula and a Cambodian army base, is perhaps the most popular of Sihanoukville's seaside attractions, with a wide strip of white sand, shady palm trees and several good seafood restaurants. Finally Ochheuteal Beach, stretching away to the south of the town, is around 3km (2 miles) long, still relatively undeveloped and very tranquil.

There are a number of offshore islands which can be visited by arrangement with one of several companies offering reasonably priced boat charters. Locals divide these islands into three groups: the Kompong Som Islands which lie close to the west of the port within an easy half-day's trip. The Ream Islands are scattered to the east towards the fishing village of Phsar Ream. Finally and more distantly, the Koh Tang Islands lie further out to sea, between four and eight hours' journey from Sihanoukville by boat. Local dive companies recommend the Kompong Som group, and more especially Koh Kaong Kang together with Koh Rong Samloem, for swimming and snorkelling when the prevailing winds are from the southwest (March to October). The Ream Group, which is more protected by the bulk of the mainland, is a better bet during the cool season (November to February) when the winds blow

Golden Lions monument, Sihanoukville

Deserted beach near Sihanoukville

from the north. For snorkelling, the waters around Koh Chraloh, Koh Ta Kiev and Koh Khteah are recommended.

Sihanoukville has numerous hotels and guesthouses of all classes, with numbers and quality increasing all the time. The city's restaurants offer a wide choice of cuisine from seafood – the local speciality – through Chinese, Vietnamese, French, Italian and even a British pub or two. Visitors should note that Sihanoukville is a surprisingly spread out place. The town centre is not particularly attractive and utterly devoid of any historical or cultural buildings, but it is the best place to look for accommodation, restaurants, shopping and transport to the beaches, all of which are some distance away. A less central but more attractive alternative is to stay out at one of the beaches. Ochheuteal offers the best standards of food and accommodation, whilst Victory is popular with backpackers and budget travellers.

230km (143 miles) from Phnom Penh on National Highway 4. Regular air-con buses take four hours.

Drive: The south coast circuit

It's an easy and pleasant drive south along Highway 3 via the quiet fishing town of Kampot and the old hill station of Bokor to Cambodia's main port and coastal centre, Sihanoukville – also known as Kompong Som. The journey back to Phnom Penh is similarly easy now that Highway 4, which crosses the beautiful Dâmrei Mountains, has been completely upgraded.

The 600km (375 mile) drive itself takes the best part of a day, but how many days you stay on the coast is up to you.

Head south from Phnom Penh along Highway 3 for 148km (92 miles), passing through the small towns of Angk Tasaom and Phumi Chhuk.

1 Kampot

Kampot (*see pp65–6*), capital of the province of the same name, is a small, relaxed town. Just 5km (3 miles) inland, by the banks of the Sanke River, there is a coastal feel to the place which adds to its rather languid attraction. *Drive east from Kampot for 25km (16 miles) along the narrow coastal road past palm trees and rice fields.*

2 Kep

Originally developed by the French as 'Kep-sur-Mer' in 1908, this small seaside resort (*see pp66–7*) near the Vietnamese frontier was utterly devastated by the Khmer Rouge. Today it offers a quieter sojourn than its chief rival, Sihanoukville, which is both larger and has some nightlife.

Retrace the route from Kep to Kampot and continue along the coastal road towards Sihanoukville. After 10km (6 miles) turn north into the Dâmrei Mountains for a further 25km (16 miles) to reach Bokor.

3 Bokor

This old hill station suffered badly during the war years, and was more or less destroyed during the Vietnamese invasion of 1979. Long little more than a ghost town, it now boasts a well-restored colonial-style hotel. *Retrace your route from Bokor to the coastal road, turn right, and continue for 95km (59 miles) to Sihanoukville.*

4 Sihanoukville

Sihanoukville (*see pp67–9*), Cambodia's only deep water port, was founded as recently as 1964 to avoid the Vietnamese stranglehold on the lower Mekong, Phnom Penh's only access to the sea. Like all other Cambodian towns it was depopulated by the Khmer Rouge, but is today a city of almost 350,000 people, as well as Cambodia's most important coastal resort.

Head north from Sihanoukville along Highway 4 for about 87km (54 miles), then turn left and follow the new coastal road (Highway 48) to Koh Kong for a further 12km (7½ miles).

5 Sre Ambel

Although known chiefly as a smugglers' port, Sre Ambel has recently begun to develop as a base for exploring the surrounding Dâmrei and Cardamon Mountains (*see pp72–3*). Local 'Extreme Cardamoms' destinations include Peal Rong Waterfall, jungle trekking and bird-watching expeditions.

Drive back from Sre Ambel to Highway 4, and continue northeast for 75km (47 miles) to Trang Tro Yeung. Turn left (west) into the hills and continue along the signposted road for a further 26km (16 miles).

6 Kirirom

The former French hill station of Kirirom was reconstituted in 1993 as Cambodia's first national park, covering an area of 350sq km (135sq miles). Located 800m (2,625ft) above sea level, it is celebrated for its cool climate, pine tree covered hills, lakes and waterfalls.

To return to Phnom Penh, return to Trang Tro Yeung and follow Highway 4 northeast for a further 90km (56 miles).

Drive: The south coast circuit

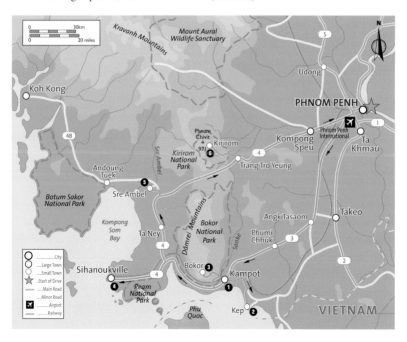

The Cardamom Mountains

The Cardamom Mountains, called Phnom Kravanh in Khmer, are Cambodia's 'final frontier' in that they are largely uninhabited and crossed by no major roads, only a few unsealed dirt tracks. Densely covered with largely impenetrable rainforest, they extend over an area of 4½ million ha (11 million acres), covering much of southwest Cambodia and extending into Thailand – where they are called the Soi Dao Mountains – at their western extremity.

In the south they meet the Dâmrei Mountains (Elephant Mountains), where the hill stations of Kirirom (see p71) and Bokor (see p65) offer cool relief from the heat of the plains. Together these conjoined ranges effectively cut off Koh Kong Province in the west from the rest of Cambodia. Mount Aural, at 1,813m (5,948ft), is the highest peak in the Cardamoms, and also the highest mountain in Cambodia.

The remote and uninhabited nature of the Cardamoms has long made them a hiding place for bandits and those seeking refuge. During the Khmer Rouge years thousands of refugees fled into the mountains, where most died, though some managed to escape to Thailand. After the fall of the Khmer Rouge regime in 1979, KR soldiers in turn made the Cardamoms into a guerrilla zone where the Vietnamese ventured at peril. The range remained one of the last Khmer Rouge base areas until the movement's eventual dissolution in 1999.

Today the Cardamoms are at peace, but remain mainland Southeast Asia's least known and least visited area of virgin rainforest. In 1993 King Norodom Sihanouk decreed the establishment of two national parks in the area, Mount Samkos Wildlife Sanctuary in the west of the range and Mount Aural Wildlife Sanctuary in the east. No infrastructure was established, however, and the areas designated were identified by aerial photographs alone. The Cardamoms are home to at least 14 endangered species including the Asian elephant, Indochinese tiger, Malayan sun bear, pileated gibbon, Siamese crocodile and royal turtle. The pristine nature of the area is under threat from illegal logging, wildlife poaching and fires started by slash-and-burn agriculture. Also threatened is the way of life of the aboriginal Pear negritos, one of Cambodia's smallest and least-known minority groups.

The Cardamom Mountains are very wet, as the peaks rise to catch the heavy rainfall of the southwest monsoon. Annual rainfall can reach nearly 500cm (200in) in some places. As a consequence, the rainforest in these areas is densely covered with foliage. In the lower elevations, tall trees reach more than 30m (100ft) in height, permitting sufficient light to filter through to a lower canopy of palm, rattan and giant ferns. Shrubs, vines and lianas thrive beneath this.

In recent years the very isolation of the Cardamoms has led to a nascent tourist industry in the area offering organised expeditions from Sre Ambel, a small and isolated town about 110km (68 miles) north of Sihanoukville. Other similar ventures are certain to follow in areas like Koh Kong. As they are organised on a deliberately 'eco-friendly' basis, these 'extreme tours' should eventually benefit the people and wildlife of the Cardamoms.

The Cardamom Mountains overlooking an isolated stream

Angkor

Asked to picture Cambodia, and it is Angkor – whether someone knows the name or not – that often comes to mind. The area is teeming with the resplendent temples that encapsulate the country's history, a legacy of Angkor's time as seat of the Khmer Empire, from around the 9th to the 15th centuries. The beauty and importance of the ancient city has earned it a place on UNESCO's World Heritage List.

Entrance to the site is very strictly controlled. All visitors must enter via the Angkor Archaeological Park Toll Gate. You can buy tickets – which permit access to all temples – for one, three or seven days. You will be issued with a pass with your photograph on it (taken digitally at the Toll Gate) and you have to show this to guards at each and every temple. Lose it and you have to buy another. General visiting hours are 5am–6pm, with the following exceptions: Banteay Srei, which closes at 5pm, and Kbal Spean, open until 3pm.

Siem Reap

Siem Reap is the centre for people visiting the nearby temples of Angkor, as well as the international and domestic air gateway to the complex. It's still not a big or terribly busy place, but is expanding fast, with a new, five-star hotel seemingly going up every few months, and many comfortable and reasonably priced smaller hotels and guesthouses. It is also a good place to eat, with a whole range of restaurants and cafés serving all kinds of cuisines, Asian, European and international.

Siem Reap is also a relaxing and welcoming town, pleasantly shaded in the vicinity of the river, still unaffected by heavy traffic and with a very friendly population, many of whom speak reasonable English. Most visitors initially enter Siem Reap from the west having landed at the nearby international airport. The road passes through paddy fields and past clumps of sugar palms, past an ever-increasing line of luxurious new hotels, some of which would not seem out of place in Las Vegas, before reaching the **Royal Independence Gardens** on the left bank of the gently flowing Siem Reap River.

To the north of this small park stands the celebrated Raffles Grand Hotel d'Angkor, while to the south is King Sihanouk's villa, though he rarely stays there. To the east is a small roundabout with a statue of the Hindu god Vishnu. A left turn here, heading north, leads

Siem Reap

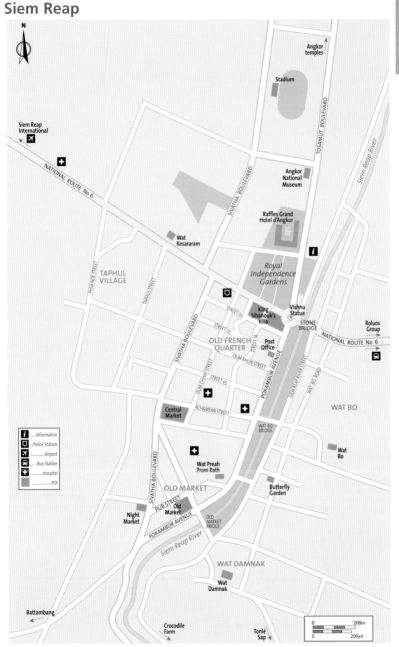

SIAM DEFEATED

Siem Reap means 'Siam Defeated', reflecting the many centuries of warfare between the Cambodians and their near neighbours, the Thais. When the first independent Thai kingdoms were established at Sukhothai (1238) and Chiang Mai (1296), the Khmer Empire was already slowly beginning to decline. The Thais spread south, establishing a kingdom at Ayutthaya in 1350. This new Thai entity began a series of attacks on Cambodia, sacking Angkor on four separate occasions between 1351 and 1431, eventually forcing the Khmers, now greatly weakened, to move their political centre south and east, towards Phnom Penh. 'Siam Defeated', therefore, seems to be something of a misnomer – but from a Cambodian perspective, Angkor returned definitively to Khmer rule in the mid-19th century, so the Thais were, finally, excluded.

directly to the Angkor temples. Straight ahead, across the river, is the dusty commercial district with the town's main fresh food market. Southwards,

along the bank of the river, leads directly to the delightful Old French Quarter, which has been widely restored and redeveloped in recent years. Just south is the bustling Old Market, one of the best places in town to buy souvenirs of Angkor. It's also a good area to relax after a day's temple watching, with many restaurants, bars and cafés, especially along and around 'Pub Street'.

Visitors come to Siem Reap to see Angkor, and Siem Reap is quite overshadowed by the glory of the massive temple complex. The town thrives not because of its attractions or rather bucolic nightlife, but because of its role as a base for visiting Angkor. This can be quite an exhausting, as well as exhilarating, experience, and the best that Siem Reap has to offer is good food, accommodation and a quiet evening stroll by the banks of the river south of the town centre.

Waterwheels on Siem Reap River

Pineapples and watermelons at a Battambang market

314km (195 miles) northwest of Phnom Penh. Siem Reap has an international airport with regular flights from Phnom Penh, Bangkok and Singapore. A flight from Phnom Penh takes 45 minutes. Air-con buses leave Phnom Penh between 6.30am and 12.30pm and take about five hours. Daily express boats from Phnom Penh take six hours.

Siem Reap environs

If the visitor has time and is adventurous, Cambodia has much to offer off the beaten track of Phnom Penh, Angkor and Sihanoukville. The Mekong and Tonlé Sap river systems are vast and mysterious, yielding opportunities for exploration unparalleled elsewhere in mainland Southeast Asia. Boat journeys here lead through submerged forests, past floating villages and stilt houses to visit bird sanctuaries and look for rare Irrawaddy dolphins or giant Mekong catfish.

The attractive riverside town of Battambang has a population of around 250,000, yet it remains bucolic, appealing and far off most tourist maps. It offers a window into Cambodia's colonial past, with some of the finest French architecture in the country, as well as an opportunity for languid relaxation. By contrast in the far north of the country, so close to the Thai border that it is almost in Thailand, the ancient 10th–12th-century temple of Preah Vihear stands high on the Dangrek escarpment, affording magnificent views of the Cambodian plains 600m (1,970ft) below (*see pp52–3*).

Battambang

Battambang, located on the left bank of the Sangker River in western Cambodia, is the country's second largest city, but remains somehow off the beaten track, a tranquil and attractive town of colonial period buildings and Chinese shop houses. Founded in the 11th century, it was ruled by neighbouring Thailand for much of its history, and Thai is more widely spoken here than in Phnom Penh or other regions to the east.

Battambang has a number of attractions beside its laid-back feel and colonial architecture (*see box*), including two old temples, Wat Tahm Rai Saw and Wat Phephittam, both dating from the mid-19th century. A small Chinese temple by the riverside near the junction of Street 1 and Street 2 is an attractive reminder of the city's ethnic

COLONIAL ARCHITECTURE

French colonial administrative buildings, shop houses and bungalows distinguish towns throughout Cambodia, but seem to survive in greater numbers in sleepy Battambang than just about anywhere else in the country, especially by the riverfront and Psar Nath. Colonial shop houses are characterised by shady colonnaded walkways, overhanging balconies, shuttered windows and pitched roofs with coloured tiles. Many are now being restored, lending a graceful feel to Battambang's downtown area.

Chinese community which is very active in local commerce. An interestingly different way to see the city is to take a boat trip along the Sangker River from the dock to the north Spean Thmei, the new stone bridge. The town's main

Stilt houses on the Tonlé Sap

market, Psar Nath, designed in Art Deco style and painted pale yellow with two white clock towers, bustles with local trade, and there is a small **Provincial Museum** at the south end of Street 1 by the riverfront that houses a fairly impressive collection of Angkor and pre-Angkor artefacts.

293km (182 miles) northwest of Phnom Penh on National Highway 5. Several daily air-con buses make the five-hour trip. 171km (106 miles) west of Siem Reap. Regular daily boats from Siem Reap take between four and seven hours. Battambang Provincial Museum, open: Mon–Fri 8–11am, 2–5pm. Admission charge.

Tonlé Sap

The Tonlé Sap (Great Lake), surrounded by a fertile rice-growing plain, dominates Cambodia's central northwest. Lying at the heart of the country's rich agricultural and fishing economies, it is the riverine 'lung' on which much of Cambodia's national prosperity depends.

The Sap River runs from the lake's southeastern rim to join the Mekong and Bassac Rivers at Phnom Penh, some 100km (62 miles) distant. The annual flooding of the Tonlé Sap makes the lake an incredibly rich source of fish snails, snakes, frogs and all manner of aquatic wildlife, whilst the farmland around the lake benefits from an annual deluge of rich sediment. The rise and fall of the waters is quite marked, and lakeside housing – which may very well be several hundred metres into the lake

during high water – is supported by stilts which may be up to 10m (33ft) high. This gives Tonlé Sap villages a surreal feel during the dry season, and a very tranquil and bucolic air when the lake is flooded and they appear to be almost floating on the water.

One of the stranger aspects of the annual flooding of the great lake has been the evolution of 'floating rice'. Before flooding occurs, rice seed is spread on the ground without any preparation of the soil. The floating rice is harvested nine months later, when the stems have grown to 3–4m (10–13ft) in response to the peak of the flood, so that the grain heads remain above water. 'Floating rice' has a relatively low yield, but it can be grown inexpensively on land for which there is no other use.

12km (7½ miles) south of Siem Reap. Taxis from Siem Reap drop off at the port of Chong Kneas where it is possible to hire a boat.

THE TONLÉ SAP FLOODPLAIN

During the dry months, roughly between November and May, the lake is at its smallest, though it still covers 2,500 to 3,000sq km (965 to 1,158sq miles). When the rains fall, however, from mid-May through October, the rising waters of the Mekong cause the flow of the Sap River to reverse. During this period, the Tonlé Sap increases in surface area, sometimes to well in excess of 10,000sq km (3,861sq miles). At its lowest most of the lake is less than 2m (6½ft) deep, and can resemble a marsh criss-crossed by navigable channels, but when at its fullest, its depth increases to as much as 14m (46ft), and it gains up to 70km (44 miles) in width.

Boat tour: Tonlé Sap

A tour of Cambodia's 'Great Lake' makes for a very different excursion from Angkor, encompassing visits to a hilltop temple, floating villages, bird sanctuaries, flooded forests and fishing opportunities. You either hire a boat privately through a travel agent in Siem Reap, or take one of the organised tours available.

Allow one day for this tour. The total distance will be between 45 and 75km (28 and 47 miles).

Drive south from Siem Reap for 11km (7 miles), following the right bank of the Siem Reap River to Phnom Krom.

1 Phnom Krom

Phnom Krom is a late 9th-century temple built by Yasovarman I (899–910) atop a 140m (450ft) hill at the western end of Tonlé Sap. A Hindu temple dedicated to the three gods Shiva, Vishnu and Brahma, it is partially collapsed but offers fine views across Chong Kneas village and the lake below.

Chong Kneas river port lies at the end of the causeway about 1.5km (1 mile) beyond Phnom Krom.

2 Chong Kneas

Chong Kneas is little more than a collection of stilt houses and moored vessels lining the last 800m (2,620ft) of the causeway leading out to the river lakeside for Siem Reap. If you are organising your own boat transport, this is the place to come.

Chong Kneas floating village lies a few hundred metres to the south and west of the causeway.

3 Chong Kneas floating village

The 'village' consists of a fairly wide main thoroughfare, with many narrow passages between houseboats, stilt houses and extensive fish traps. The inhabitants are mainly ethnic Vietnamese. There's a police station, two or three floating petrol stations, floating restaurants and, surprisingly, floating pigsties. The **Gecko Environment Centre** (*open: around 8am–6pm*) offers displays and information on the ecology and biodiversity of the lake area.

The bird sanctuary is at the western end of Tonlé Sap about 18km (11 miles) by boat from Chong Kneas.

4 Prek Toal Bird Sanctuary

The bird sanctuary at the Prek Toal Biosphere is one of the most important breeding grounds in Southeast Asia for large aquatic birds. The biosphere

covers more than 30,000 ha (74,000 acres) at the northwest tip of Tonlé Sap and is home to many species including the black-headed ibis, painted stork, milky stork, spot-billed pelican and grey-headed fish eagle.
Admission charge.
Kompong Phluk is 34km (21 miles) east of Prek Toal Bird Sanctuary.

5 Kompong Phluk

Kompong Phluk is a group of three large stilt house villages standing on the floodplain of the Tonlé Sap. The villagers, who number about 3,000 between the villages, are primarily Khmer. Flooded mangrove forest surrounds the area and is home to a wide variety of wildlife including crab-eating macaques.

Kompong Khleang is about 36km (22 miles) east of Chong Kneas, or about 20km (12 miles) east of Prek Toal Bird Sanctuary.

6 Kompong Khleang

Kompong Khleang is located on the northern lake-edge east of Siem Reap town. Although it is one of the largest settlements on the lake, it gets only a small number of visitors. During the rainy season, the waters of the lake rise to within a metre of the houses, but during the dry season, when the waters retreat, the stilt houses rise up to 10m (33ft) from the marshy ground.
The boat will bring you back to the pier at Chong Kneas, from where you can take a taxi back to Siem Reap.

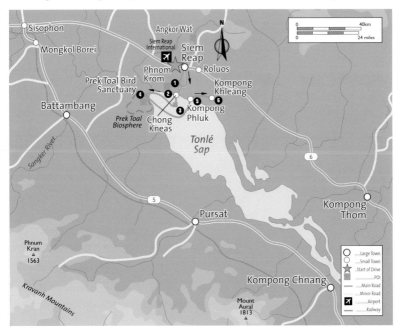

Zhou Daguan

A Chinese envoy, Zhou Daguan, visited Angkor in 1296, and left a remarkable record of his impressions. He records that 'the walled city of Angkor was some 16 li (8km/5 miles) in circumference. It had five gates, with five portals. Outside the wall stretched a great moat across which massive causeways gave access to the city. The Royal Palace, as well as the official buildings and homes of the nobles, all face east.'

He continues: 'I have heard it said that within the palace are many marvellous sights, but these are so strictly guarded that I had no chance to see them. Out of the palace rises a golden tower, to the top of which the ruler ascends nightly to sleep.' By contrast, the houses of the ordinary folk were thatched with straw, for 'no one would venture to vie with the nobility'.

Zhou was fascinated by King Indravarman III (1296–1308), whom he met on five occasions. His description is most evocative: 'When the king goes out, troops are at the head of the escort; then follow flags, banners and music. Palace women, numbering from three to five hundred, wearing flowered cloth, with flowers in their hair, hold candles in their hands and form a troupe. Even in broad daylight,

We are indebted to Zhou Daguan for his invaluable descriptions of Angkor

the candles are lighted. Then follow other palace women, bearing royal paraphernalia made of gold and silver… Ministers and princes are mounted on elephants, and in front of them one can see, from afar, innumerable red umbrellas. Next come the wives and concubines of the king, in palanquins, carriages, on horseback, and on elephants. Behind them comes the king, standing on an elephant, holding a sacred sword in his hand. The elephant's tusks are encased in gold.'

Angkor was a society rigidly stratified by class. At the base, and vital for building and irrigation work, were the slaves. This group could not sleep in houses, though they could lie beneath them. On entering a house, they had to prostrate themselves before starting work. Slaves had no civil rights, their marriages were not recognised by the state, and they were obliged to call their owners 'father' and 'mother'. They often tried to run away, and when caught would be tattooed, mutilated and shackled.

Above the slaves stood a number of intermediate classes who were free, but not part of the nobility. These included private slave-owners, landholders and merchants. Zhou adds: 'In this country, it is the women who are concerned with commerce… Every day a market takes place which begins at six in the morning and ends

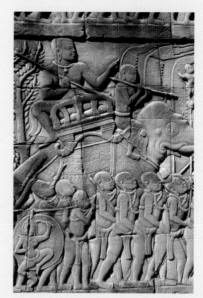

Engravings representing a military procession, Angkor Thom

at noon. There is no market made up of shops where people live. Instead people use a piece of matting, which they spread out on the earth. Each of them has her own position, and I believe that fees are charged for these locations.'

Zhou mentions three religious traditions established at Angkor. These were Brahmanism, Buddhism and Shaivism. Of the Buddhist monks, he writes: 'they shave their heads and wear yellow robes, leaving the right shoulder bare. For the lower part of the body they wear a yellow skirt. They go barefoot.' It is a description that applies equally well today.

Angkor Thom

Angkor Thom, which means 'Great City' in Khmer, dates from the late 12th century and was founded by King Jayavarman VII (1181–1220). At its peak, it was not just the largest city in the Khmer Empire, but quite probably anywhere in the world, with a population estimated at around one million people. The city was protected by a square, 8m (26ft) high wall about 12km (7½ miles) in extent, surrounded by a wide moat.

Angkor Wat

Angkor Wat is the single largest religious monument in the world. Based on a model of the Hindu universe centred on a stylised Mount Meru, it is said that the complex required as much stone as the Great Pyramid of Cheops in Egypt. Yet Angkor Wat is also exquisitely carved with 600m (1,968ft) of bas-reliefs recounting tales from Hindu mythology, as well as around 2,000 *apsara* or celestial dancing girls.

Built during the 12th century by King Surayavarman II (1113–50), Angkor Wat means literally 'the City which is a Temple'. It was established as a Hindu temple dedicated to Shiva, but it was also intended as a mausoleum for Surayavarman II. Its orientation is different from other temples at Angkor, as the main entrance is from the west – the direction of sunset, associated with death – rather than from the east. The bas-reliefs may most conveniently be viewed by proceeding anticlockwise from the Shiva statue in the west entrance.

The massive scale of Angkor is difficult to grasp. Just walking to the central shrine across the moat and along the main causeway is awe-inspiring. At the end the main towers of the temple rise 65m (213ft) through three separate levels. Atop the third level there are five great towers, one at each corner, and the great central spire. The towers are conical in shape, representing lotus flowers. The area of land covered by the complex is around 210 hectares (519 acres) surrounded by a moat which is 200m (656ft) wide. While the central tower represents Mount Meru, located at the centre of the universe, the outer walls symbolise the mountains at the edge of the world, and the surrounding moats the oceans beyond.

The great causeway leads to the main temple complex, passing two cruciform buildings styled 'libraries', and two large reservoirs or tanks, at least one of which is generally filled with water, offering fine opportunities to photograph the five central towers reflected amid lotus flowers. At the entrance to the first level there is a large standing stone figure of an eight-armed Vishnu. In recent times, however, a Buddha head has replaced that of Vishnu, and the statue is now much venerated by Cambodian Buddhists.

The first level is distinguished by a succession of amazing stone panels carved in bas-relief. In the **West Gallery** these represent the **Battle of Lanka**,

Vendors and visitors, Angkor Wat

depicting the long struggle between Lord Rama and Ravana, the demon-king of Lanka, for possession of Sita. The panel is distinguished by fine representations of Hanuman's monkey army, and the **Battle of Kurukshetra**, a scene from the great Hindu epic the *Mahabharata* in which the opposing Kauravas and Pandavas clash with each other. Foot soldiers are at the lowest level, with officers on elephant back and in the upper tiers.

The **South Gallery** panels represent the **Army of King Surayavarman II** in triumphal march. The king rides a war elephant and carries a battleaxe. He is shaded by 15 umbrellas and fanned by numerous servants. Contrasting with the ordered ranks of Khmer soldiers, a group of Thai mercenaries march out of step and wear sarongs. Next come **Scenes of Heaven and Hell,** depicting the punishments of hell and rewards of heaven. Those who have accumulated merit in life seem to approach Yama, the God of the Underworld, and are offered passage to heaven. Below them, sinners are dragged to hell by hideous demons wielding heavy clubs.

The **East Gallery** boasts the most famous bas-relief in Angkor, the **Churning of the Ocean of Milk.** In one vast, magnificently carved panel, 88 *asura* (devils) on the left and 92 *deva* (gods) on the right (north side) churn the sea of milk with a giant serpent for

Battle scene, West Gallery, Angkor Wat

1,000 years. Their purpose is to create the elixir of immortality, which both sides desire. Overhead, finely carved *apsara* sing and dance to encourage the gods and devils in their labour. This is followed by the **Victory of Vishnu over the Demons** where Vishnu, riding on a *garuda* (a mythical bird-like creature), is engaged in victorious combat against a legion of demons.

The **North Gallery** represents the **Victory of Krishna over Bana**. Here Vishnu, incarnated as Krishna, attacks the city of Bana, the demon-king subdues Bana, then mercifully kneels before Shiva and asks that the life of Bana be spared. This is followed by the **Battle between the Gods and the Demons**, an exquisitely carved panel where the Hindu gods overcome numerous devils. Once again, Vishnu rides a *garuda* (a mythical bird-like creature), while Shiva rides a sacred goose.

The second level is reached from the west entrance by a steep flight of steps. This is the 'cruciform cloister', with four deep stone tanks (now dry) that once used to hold lustral water for the ritual purification of priests and members of the royal family. The surrounding walls are covered with beautifully executed carvings of standing *apsara*, and there are numbers of stone Buddha images introduced after the temple's rededication to Buddhism, many badly damaged in the intervening centuries.

In times past, only kings and high priests were permitted access to the

Carvings representing *apsara*, upper galleries, Angkor Wat

third level. Here the central tower rises 42m (138ft) above the upper level, bringing the overall height of the central sanctuary at Angkor to 65m (213ft), or about the same height as the Cathedral of Notre Dame in Paris. There are four richly decorated porches opening to the cardinal directions, all of which once gave access to a central statue of Vishnu – perhaps the one standing today in the west entrance. Today, in Theravada Buddhist Cambodia, this has been replaced with a modern image of the Buddha.

The central sanctuary and the third level of Angkor are best visited at sunrise or sunset. Wonderful views are seen across the entire temple, and it is easier to grasp the huge size of the entire complex. Towards sunset, rays of sunlight pass through the elaborately carved sandstone windows, illuminating the best-preserved and most exquisite *apsara* in warm, gold-and-red hues.

Walk: Around Angkor Wat

The temple rises through three levels to a cruciform central shrine. The finest bas-reliefs are found on the first level, notably in the South and East Galleries. A statue of Vishnu dominates the West Entrance Hall. The most exquisite apsara *are found on the topmost level.*

Allow at least half a day for this walk, a full day if you are a temple enthusiast.

Unusually amongst Khmer temples, Angkor faces west, and the main entrance is via the Western Causeway, leading across the moat, between two restored library buildings and nearby ponds, directly to the main entrance of the temple itself.

1 The Western Causeway

The approach to the main temple sanctuary is along a raised path approximately 350m (1,150ft) long by 9m (30ft) wide. This causeway is flanked by snake-like *naga* balustrades on either side. Two buildings, sometimes described as 'libraries', stand on either side of the causeway.
Walk east along the causeway to the main entrance.

2 The West Gallery

The West Gallery shelters a standing statue of Vishnu with eight arms, now venerated by local Buddhists. The bas-reliefs of the south section of the West Gallery represent the Battle of Kurukshetra.

Turn right by the figure of Vishnu and walk to the southwest corner of Angkor Wat.

3 The South Gallery

This gallery contains two outstanding bas-relief panels, the Army of King Surayavarman II and Scenes of Heaven and Hell. The original panelled ceiling has been restored at the eastern end of this gallery, but in concrete rather than wood.
Continue along the gallery to the southeast corner of Angkor Wat, then turn left (north).

4 The East Gallery

Once again, there are two outstanding bas-relief panels in this gallery, the first – the Churning of the Ocean of Milk – being the most celebrated in all Angkor. Beyond this is a long panel representing the Victory of Vishnu over the Demons.
Continue past the 'Elephant Gate' to the northeast corner of Angkor Wat, then turn left (west).

5 The North Gallery

The bas-reliefs here represent the Victory of Krishna over Bana, and the Battle between the Gods and the Demons. The gods are distinguishable by their traditional mounts and aspects. Shiva, for example, rides a sacred goose, whilst Vishnu has four arms and is seated on a *garuda*.

Continue to the northwest corner of Angkor Wat, then turn south and walk back to the standing figure of Vishnu. Climb the stone stairs to the second level.

6 The second level

The second level is constructed in a cruciform, with four stone tanks once filled with sacred water used for bathing by priests and initiates. The walls are lined with an astonishing number of beautifully executed *apsara* dancers.

Follow the signs indicating an anticlockwise circuit of the central tower until you return to the main steps leading to the third level.

7 The third level

This final level represents the summit of Mount Meru, supporting a central tower and four surrounding towers. The views from the summit are remarkable, as are the fine carvings of *apsara* and *devata*.

Descend to the west following the signs and exit via the main entrance and Western Causeway.

Walk: Around Angkor Wat

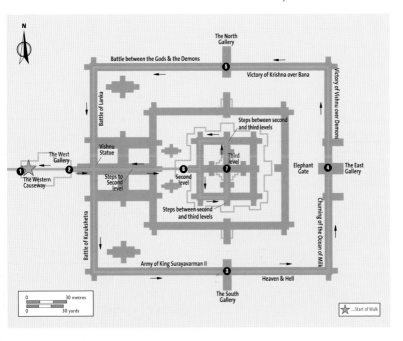

Baphuon

Baphuon is a three-tiered temple mountain built in the 11th century by King Udayadityavarman II (1050–66). It represents Mount Meru, and was dedicated to the Hindu god Shiva. A central tower with four entrances once stood at the summit. In its days of glory it would have been 50m (164ft) high, and it certainly made an impression on the Chinese visitor Zhou Daguan (*see pp82–3*), who described it in 1297 as 'a tower of bronze… a truly astonishing spectacle, with more than ten chambers at its base'. It is sufficiently important to have given its name to an 11th-century style of Khmer architecture (*see pp94–5*). In the 15th century Baphuon was rededicated to Buddhism, and a 9m by 70m (30ft by 230ft) reclining Buddha was added to the temple's second level on the west side.

The Bayon, Angkor Thom

Baphuon has long since collapsed, however, probably because the massive central tower rested on sandy ground. The École Française d'Extrême Orient began the process of carrying out restoration as long ago as 1960, but had to abandon the project when the Second Indochina War spilled over into Cambodia and made the effort too risky. Restoration started again in 1995, again under the guidance of French archaeologists, and until 2006 visitor access was restricted. It is now possible to visit much of Baphuon, though restoration is not scheduled for completion until around 2009. It is reached by a raised causeway some 200m (220yd) long.

The Bayon

This is, together with Angkor Wat and the forest temple of Ta Prohm, the most celebrated of all the monuments at Angkor. A crumbling, many-faced temple, it has become synonymous with the ancient civilisation of Angkor, and exudes an almost palpable air of mystery.

Situated at the centre of Angkor Thom, the Bayon was built in the 13th century by King Jayavarman VII, 'The Builder' (*see box p95*), and must be considered the most extraordinary structure at Angkor after Angkor Wat. Until the discovery of a figure of Bodhisattva Avalokitesvara here in 1925, the Bayon was thought to be a Hindu temple dating from the 10th century. It is now considered to be a 13th-century

Buddhist temple built atop an earlier temple that was probably Hindu. Jayavarman VII, who was a pious Mahayana Buddhist, created 54 towers bearing more than 200 huge, enigmatic stone faces, believed to represent Bodhisattva Avalokitesvara, and almost certainly carved in the likeness of Jayavarman VII.

The Bayon is a symbolic Mount Meru, rising on three levels, and accessed through eight cruciform gateways. These are linked by galleries that were once covered with stone roofs and which are gradually being restored. These galleries contain some of the most remarkable bas-reliefs at Angkor, featuring everyday scenes as well as panels of battles, especially with the Cham. The domestic scenes are particularly informative, representing market scenes, festivals, cockfights, women giving birth, people playing games, hunters, fishermen and so on. There are also representations of scenes at the royal court, including entertainments staged by wrestlers, sword fighters and dancing girls.

The East Gallery features a military procession of the Khmer army, with elephants, ox carts, horsemen and musicians. Parasols shield the senior commanders, including Jayavarman VII himself. The South Gallery bas-reliefs depict a great naval battle that took place on the nearby Tonlé Sap in 1177 between the Khmer and the invading Cham. The Khmer warriors wear their hair short, while the Cham sport long

Face in the Bayon, Angkor Thom

hair and helmets. Giant fish and crocodiles devour the bodies of warriors falling from the boats. The Khmers were victorious, and at the end of the South Gallery Jayavarman VII is represented in triumphant victory.

The North Gallery depicts entertainers such as acrobats and jugglers at the royal court, perhaps celebrating after victory. The Interior Galleries feature more battles between the Cham and Khmer, as well as war elephants and more scenes from everyday life in 13th-century Angkor, but the real attraction of the second- and third-level galleries are the sublime and somewhat eerie representations of Jayavarman VII as *Bodhisattva*.

Bike tour: Angkor Thom

Cycling is an ideal way to explore the ancient city of Angkor Thom. Distances are not too great, and the traffic is light. You are as likely to encounter an elephant as a minibus. This 16km (10-mile) tour encompasses the most important temples and sights of Angkor Thom, including the South Gate, the Bayon, Baphuon, Phimeanakas, the Elephant Terrace, the Terrace of the Leper King and the Khleangs.

Allow one day for the tour.

Start at the South Gate.

1 The South Gate

There are five gates into the city, each approached by a causeway across the moat. The South Gate is the best preserved and most impressive. One hundred and eight stone figures flank the causeway, fifty-four gods on the left and the same number of demons on the right. Both gods and demons support great *naga* snakes on their knees. At the start of the causeway these *naga* raise their nine heads in a fan-shaped motif. The South Gate also bears four huge enigmatic faces, thought to be likenesses of Jayavarman VII.

Cycle through the South Gate and continue north for 1¼ km (¾ mile) to the Bayon.

2 The Bayon

This is the most impressive temple at Angkor Thom and, after Angkor Wat, in the whole Angkor complex. Built by Jayavarman VII, it is currently undergoing major restoration by the Japanese.

Cycle north from the Bayon for 200m (220yd). The main entrance to Baphuon is on the left.

3 Baphuon

One of the oldest buildings in Angkor Thom, Baphuon predates the founding of the present walled city. Approach by way of a 200m (220yd) long raised causeway of laterite.

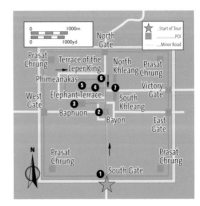

Leave Baphuon by the main entrance. The south end of the Elephant Terrace is immediately to the left.

4 The Elephant Terrace

Built by the Buddhist monarch Jayavarman VII, this structure is over 300m (330yd) long, and stretches from the Baphuon to the nearby Terrace of the Leper King.

Halfway along the Elephant Terrace, opposite the Avenue of Victory, turn left to enter Phimeanakas.

5 Phimeanakas

Immediately to the north of Baphuon stands the badly decayed royal palace enclosure, currently undergoing restoration. The most important structure here is Phimeanakas, the 'Celestial Palace'. Built during the 10th–11th centuries, it was the work of several kings but was founded by King Rajendravarman II (941–68).

Leave Phimeanakas by the main entrance, and continue north along the Elephant Terrace. Walk through the concealed passage on the south side of the Terrace of the Leper King and climb the steps to the statue of the Leper King.

6 The Terrace of the Leper King

Like the Elephant Terrace, this much smaller structure dates from the late 12th century and is chiefly remarkable for its fine bas-reliefs.

The Khleangs are clearly visible to the east of the Terrace of the Leper King.

Statues at the entrance of Angkor Thom

7 The Khleangs and Prasat Suor Prat

To the east of the Terrace of the Leper King, directly across Central Square, stand the North Khleang and South Khleang, 10th-century structures that may have served as palaces.

Immediately in front of these stand 12 laterite towers called Prasat Suor Prat or 'Temple of the Tightrope Dancers'. Originally small shrines housing Hindu deities or Shiva *linga*, it is speculated that acrobats once performed for the king on ropes stretched between these towers.

Finish your ride and cycle back the way you came to the South Gate.

Angkor chronology

Khmer temple architecture has its roots in the pre-Angkorean 7th-century style of Sambor Prei Kuk which flourished in the region of Kompong Thom to the east of Angkor, and the 8th-century style of Kompong Preah, relics of which may still be found at Prasat Ak Yum by Angkor's Western Baray. Historians next identify a 'Transitional Stage', known as Kulen Style, from Mount Kulen to the northeast of Angkor.

This developed during the 8th century, and may have been influenced by the art of neighbouring Champa. As there, buildings are of brick with stone lintels, but more decorative than the earlier pre-Angkorean styles.

Angkor Period architecture is generally dated from Jayavarman II's establishment of Hariharalaya as the Khmer capital near the site of present-day Roluos at the beginning of the 9th century. From this time until the eventual 15th-century abandonment of Angkor, art historians identify ten distinct architectural styles.

875–90 Preah Ko: This style is characterised by the use of brick towers and stone lintels. Sculptured figures are larger and heavier than in pre-Angkorean traditions.

890–925 Bakheng: During this period the use of Mount Meru as a model for temple mountains evolved, often with five towers arranged in a quincunx. Bakheng is the most famous example; other examples are Phnom Bok and Phnom Krom.

921–41 Koh Ker: This short-lived style was developed during the reign of Jayavarman IV, who established a new capital at Koh Ker some 65km (40 miles) east of Angkor. Little remains of his capital, and the finest examples of Koh Ker sculptural style are Sugriva and Valin, two monkey-headed brothers from the *Ramayana*, at the National Museum in Phnom Penh (*see pp31 & 34–5*).

945–65 Pre Rup: This style, developed during the reign of Rajendravarman, builds on the Bakheng fashion with five towers arranged in a quincunx, but higher, steeper and with more tiers.

967–1000 Banteay Srei: Represented by the delicate and refined temple northeast of Angkor, this approach – which was not directly associated with royalty, but with Yajnavaraha, a counsellor to the royal court of Rajendravarman – is characterised by exquisitely ornate carvings and distinctly sensuous *apsara* and *devata* female figures.

965–1025 Khleang: An aesthetic characterised by the use of massive stone blocks and limited decoration, cruciform *gopura* gateways and long galleries.

1025–80 Baphuon: By the time Baphuon style was developed, Khmer architecture was reaching its majestic apogee. Characterised by vast proportions and long, vaulted galleries, the sculpture of the period combines increasing realism and narrative sequence.

1080–1175 Angkor Wat: Art historians generally agree that the style of Angkor Wat represents the apex of Khmer architectural and sculptural genius. The greatest of all temple mountains, it also boasts the finest bas-relief narratives with figures of *devata* (guardian spirits) and *apsara* (celestial dancing girls) both broad-hipped and full-breasted. The art of lintel-carving, too, reached its zenith.

1180–1240 Bayon: Considered a synthesis of previous modes, this – the last great Angkor architectural style – is also characterised by a detectable decline in quality. While still magnificent, there is more use of laterite and less of sandstone. There is also greater employment of Buddhist imagery, and correspondingly less of Hindu themes.

1240–1431 Post-Bayon: The chief example of this style, which is distinguished by the use of raised causeway terraces, is the Terrace of the Leper King at Angkor Thom.

1431: Angkor is sacked by the Thais, causing its population to migrate south.

JAYAVARMAN VII

King Jayavarman VII (c1181–1215) was the greatest builder in the history of Angkor. He was a Mahayana Buddhist whose professed aim was to alleviate the sufferings of his people, but one can only speculate at the cost, in human terms, of his prolific construction programme. Archaeologists identify three stages in this programme. In the first he built public infrastructure such as hospitals, rest houses, reservoirs and irrigation works including Neak Pean. Next he constructed temple mountains to honour his father at Preah Khan and his mother at Ta Prohm. Finally he built his own temple mountain at the Bayon. Collectively these form the greatest and most celebrated structures at Angkor.

Elephant and Leper King Terraces

Directly to the east of Baphuon and Phimeanakas, on the left side of the road to the North Gate, stand two terraces that are simply covered with carvings. The first and longest of these is the Elephant Terrace. Built by the amazingly prolific Jayavarman VII, this structure is over 300m (984ft) long, and stretches from Baphuon in the south to the contiguous Terrace of the Leper King in the north. It has three main raised platforms and two lower ones. The terrace is thought to have been used by the king, members of the royal family, senior ministers and generals to review the Cambodian army and also to watch spectacular entertainment. The whole terrace is elaborately decorated. Here are the carved sandstone elephants from which the terrace gets its name, and in addition tigers, lions, *naga*, *garuda*, sacred geese and lotus flowers, all represented in a wealth of detail.

Immediately to the north of the Elephant Terrace and in a direct line with it stands the Terrace of the Leper King. Like the Elephant Terrace, this much smaller structure dates from the late 12th century and is the work of the great Buddhist monarch Jayavarman VII. It is generally accepted that the statue here represents Yama, God of Judgement and Death. The original statue has been removed to the courtyard of the National Museum in Phnom Penh (*see pp31 & 34–5*) for safety, and the statue currently on top of the terrace is a replica.

Built of laterite faced with sandstone, the terrace wall is adorned with snakes, *garuda*, many-armed giants, *apsara*, soldiers, fish, elephants and flowers. When scholars from the École Française d'Extrême Orient were restoring the terrace, they discovered a collapsed inner wall which has now been restored and is accessible via a narrow passageway that is, if anything, even more elaborately carved.

Elephant Terrace, Angkor Thom

Figures on the Terrace of the Leper King, Angkor Thom

Phimeanakas

Phimeanakas was established in the mid-10th century by King Rajendravarman II (941–68). A temple mountain constructed in the Khleang style, it was built as a three-tiered pyramid with a tower on top. The tower has collapsed and is due for restoration, but the pyramid base is still accessible, and can be climbed by steep stairways. Dedicated to Hinduism, it is also associated in legend with a golden tower inside the royal palace where a nine-headed serpent lived. Each night this serpent would appear to the king as a beautiful woman, with whom the monarch would have congress before joining his wives and concubines elsewhere in the palace. It was thought that if the king failed in this obligation he would die, while by performing this duty the royal lineage of the Khmer kings was assured. This legend is recounted in the 13th-century account of Zhou Daguan (*see pp82–3*).

Although Phimeanakas is currently very dilapidated, it is worth climbing to the upper terrace to obtain an excellent view of the nearby Baphuon. Turning the other way, in a northwards direction, two former royal baths become visible. The smaller and deeper is called **Srah Srei**, or the 'Women's Bathing Place', while the

Entrance to Phimeanakas, Angkor Thom

moved his court from the capital Hariharalaya at Roluos. Phnom Bakheng is, again, a symbolic representation of Mount Meru, home to the Hindu pantheon. The temple faces east, measures 76sq m (818sq ft) at its base and is built in a pyramid form of six tiers. At the top level, five sandstone sanctuaries, in various states of repair, stand in a quincunx pattern. Originally, 108 small towers were arrayed around the temple at ground level and on the six tiers; most of these are long collapsed.

other pond, **Srah Bros**, is known as the 'Men's Bathing Place'.

Phnom Bakheng

A few hundred metres outside the South Gate of Angkor Thom, to the west side of the road, the hill of Phnom Bakheng rises 67m (220ft) above the surrounding plains. This is an ideal spot to view the distant spires of Angkor Wat at sunset, but can be ascended – with some difficulty – at any time of the day (*see box*). On the summit of the hill stand the remains of Phnom Bakheng, a 9th-century Hindu temple mountain originally dedicated to Shiva and founded by King Yasovarman (889–910). Constructed more than two centuries before Angkor Wat, Phnom Bakheng was probably, in its prime, the principal temple of Angkor. It was designed as the architectural centrepiece of a new capital, Yasodharapura, which Yasovarman constructed when he

Monumental staircase at Phimeanakas, Angkor Thom

The outer temples

While Angkor Wat can be explored on foot and Angkor Thom by bicycle, the outer temples are so widely spread that a car – or motorbike – is really essential. Yet despite the distances, a visit to the outer temples should not be missed. From the cloistered silence of Preah Khan, through the unique medicinal baths of Neak Pean, to the jungle-covered glory of numinous Ta Prohm, the outer temples are quite simply superlative.

Banteay Samré, Angkor

Banteay Samré

Roughly square in plan, Banteay Samré is a massive structure in the Angkor Wat style. It has been postulated that the name Samré is derived from a minority ethnic group who lived in the region of Phnom Kulen to the north of Angkor. There are no known inscriptions relating to the temple, but the style suggests it dates from the 12th or 13th century, and was built at around the same time as Angkor Wat, probably by Surayavarman II and his successor Yasovarman II.

A solid laterite wall surrounds the temple, with entrances at the four cardinal points. Inside, uniquely, there is a laterite-paved moat which must have appeared splendid when filled with water, though unfortunately today it is dry. The main temple complex is reached by a raised laterite causeway. The serpent balustrades on the stairs leading to the moats represent the seven-headed *naga* Muchalinda who is said to have sheltered the meditating Buddha from the elements.

Located just to the east of the massive man-made reservoir – now quite dry – known as the Eastern Baray, Banteay Samré or 'Citadel of Samré' is a little off the beaten track. Visitors making the 'Grand Circuit' (see pp102–3) should turn east after passing the East Mebon (see p102) and drive for about 2½km (1½ miles) to the edge of the Eastern Baray, then continue along an unpaved track for a further 500m (550yd).

East Mebon and Pre Rup

The East Mebon was built by Rajendravarman II (944–68) in honour of the memory of his parents. It stands on a mound that was once an artificial island at the centre of the Eastern Baray, a man-made reservoir that is now dry. It has been calculated that at the time of its construction the Eastern Baray would have held water to an average depth of 3m (10ft), with an overall volume of 40 million cubic metres (1.41 billion cubic feet) of water. Once the Eastern Mebon would have dominated this great reservoir, its towers reflected in the waters, but today it rises above rice fields and sugar palm trees.

The East Mebon was constructed as a Hindu temple in the form of an artificial mountain representing Mount Meru. Surrounded by three laterite walls, the temple rises through three levels before reaching a central platform bearing a quincunx of four small outer towers and one large central tower. The towers are of brick, with holes that formerly anchored stucco decorations clearly visible. The stone stairways at the first level are flanked by sandstone lions, while sandstone elephants dominate the corners of the second and third levels. The temple was dedicated to the god Vishnu, and the lintel of the west *gopura* bears a likeness of this deity as Narasingha, half-lion and half-man.

Like the East Mebon, nearby Pre Rup is a Hindu temple mountain dedicated to the god Shiva. Constructed in

Tower at the East Mebon, Angkor

sandstone and brick, it has a square layout and two perimeter walls. Steps lead to the top level, with carved sitting stone lions arrayed at intermediate levels. At the top, five towers are arranged in a quincunx pattern, smaller at each corner of the square and a larger one in the centre.

8km (5 miles) east of Angkor Wat.

Drive: The Grand Circuit

This drive is around 25km (16 miles) long, and takes in all the major temples in the vicinity of Angkor Wat and Angkor Thom.

The drive requires at least one full day, including the visits to the temples, and can easily be extended to two (or more) days.

Start at the North Gate of Angkor Thom and follow the road east for about 1½km (1 mile) to Preah Khan.

1 Preah Khan

The 'Temple of the Sacred Sword' was founded by Jayavarman VII to honour his father (*see pp105–7*).
Continue east from Preah Khan for 2½km (1½ miles) and turn south for 250m (275yd) at the sign for Neak Pean.

2 Neak Pean

This unique temple, also built by Jayavarman VII, served as a source of lustral water for curing the sick (*see pp104–5*).
Return to the main road and turn east for a further 2km (1¼ miles). Where the road turns south into the Eastern Baray, a short track leads north to Ta Som.

3 Ta Som

This remote and beautiful temple, dating from the late 12th century, still retains an aura of tranquillity and isolation (*see p105*).
Continue south across the Eastern Baray for 2km (1¼ miles).

4 East Mebon

This massive temple once stood on an island in the middle of the waters of the Eastern Baray. It still dominates the now dry landscape (*see p101*).
Continue south out of the Eastern Baray. After about 1½km (1 mile) on the edge of the reservoir stands Pre Rup.

5 Pre Rup

Built by Rajendravarman II, Pre Rup is a Hindu temple dedicated to the god Shiva. Rising through three levels, there are good views from the top of the monument north across the Eastern Baray towards Phnom Kulen, as well as southwest to the distant spires of Angkor Wat.
On leaving Pre Rup the road continues due west, and after 1km (²/₃ mile) runs past the great reservoir of Srah Srang.

6 Srah Srang

Srah Srang or the 'Royal Bath' was constructed as a massive tank by Jayavarman VII (*see pp110–11*). *Continue west past a turning to the left straight after Srah Srang. Banteay Kdei follows immediately.*

7 Banteay Kdei

This large Buddhist temple complex was similarly constructed on the orders of 'The Builder', Jayavarman VII (*see pp110–11*). *Continue west about 200m (220yd) from Banteay Kdei to the east gate of Ta Prohm.*

8 Ta Prohm

Built by Jayavarman VII for his mother, this complex was already famous as the 'jungle temple' before Angelina Jolie and the movie *Tomb Raider* brought it mass recognition (*see pp112–13*). *Follow the road north from the west gate of Ta Prohm for about 1½km (1 mile), to Ta Keo. Continue west towards Angkor Thom's Victory Gate; Thommanon is 750m (825yd) beyond Ta Keo on your right.*

9 Ta Keo and Thommanon

Ta Keo is a ziggurat-like artificial Mount Meru built in the late 10th and early 11th centuries by Jayavarman V and his successor Surayavarman I. Thommanon is a small Hindu temple built by Surayavarman II in the early 12th century, mainly notable for its finely carved female divinities (*see pp111–12*).

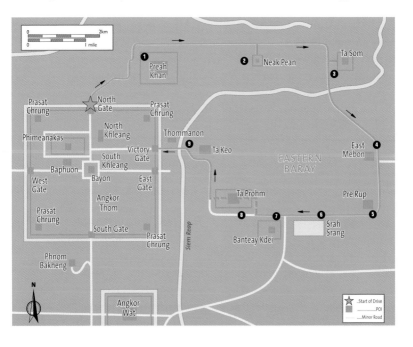

Neak Pean, Angkor

Neak Pean and Ta Som

Neak Pean, or 'Entwined Serpents', which dates from the second half of the 12th century, was built by Jayavarman VII and dedicated to Buddhism. The temple is set in an artificial pond which measures 70m (230ft) square. This central pool is surrounded at the cardinal points by four smaller square pools which are set somewhat lower. In the centre of the main pool is a circular island bearing a shrine dedicated to Avalokitesvara. Two intertwined serpents circle the base of the island, providing the complex with its name. To the east of the island is the sculpted figure of the horse Balaha, a manifestation of Avalokitesvara who transformed himself into a horse to rescue a group of shipwrecked merchants.

The central pool represents Lake Anavatapta, located at the summit of the universe, which gives birth to the four great rivers and whose waters are supposed to cure all illnesses. These rivers are represented at Neak Pean by four gargoyle-like sculpted heads through the mouths of which water once flowed from the main pool to the four smaller ones. The east head represents a human being, the south head a lion, the west head a horse and the north head an elephant. In times past sick or troubled pilgrims at Neak Pean would consult a specialist priest before going to whichever one of the four smaller pools was deemed appropriate for his or her condition. Next servants of the shrine would release a plug and allow the lustral waters of the central pool to flow through the gargoyle spout, splashing over the head and body of the ill person and hopefully effecting a cure.

Ta Som was built in the late 12th century by the Buddhist monarch Jayavarman VII, and dedicated to the memory of his father. Constructed in the Bayon style, the great appeal of this largely unrestored temple is its remote location. On the northern periphery of the Angkor Grand Circuit, it attracts relatively few visitors, and as a consequence is a tranquil oasis of birds and trees. A single shrine of one level, the temple should be entered and exited via the west gate, a cruciform *gopura* surmounted by four carved faces. The inner shrine is partly collapsed, but it is pleasant to walk through the covered galleries to the central sanctuary where the roots of strangling fig trees surmount and bind the ancient stonework. The eastern gateway, again bearing four benignly smiling stone faces, gives way to empty scrubland dotted with clumps of sugar palm trees. *About 2½km (1²/₃ miles) east of Preah Khan, a signposted track leads south for around 250m (275yd) to Neak Pean. Ta Som is about 2km (1¼ miles) to the east of Neak Pean.*

Preah Khan

Built in the style of the Bayon and dedicated to Buddhism, this vast temple was used as a monastery and teaching

Western entrance to Preah Khan, Angkor

Essai (wise men), Preah Khan, Angkor

place. It is also thought to have served Jayavarman VII as a temporary capital when he was rebuilding nearby Angkor Thom after the capture and sacking of the city by Cham invaders in 1177. At its height, Preah Khan was dedicated to Avalokitesvara and 430 lesser deities, and was fabulously wealthy, with nearly 100,000 attendants, 1,000 *apsara* dancers and 1,000 teachers, as well as stores of gold, silver, jewels and pearls.

There is an appealing quality about Preah Khan which comes from its relative tranquillity and closeness to nature. In part this is because the temple has yet to be fully restored, and huge trees with roots like melted cheese still cover large parts of the complex. The temple is much less visited than either Angkor Wat or Ta Prohm, and it is possible to lose oneself in the deserted, tumbledown halls, far from the tourist buses at nearby Angkor Wat.

An inscribed stone stele, found at Preah Khan in 1939 and removed for safekeeping to the Angkor Conservatory, indicates that the central sanctuary was dedicated in 1191, when the pious Buddhist and great builder Jayavarman VII was king of Angkor. Unfortunately, at least from an art history perspective, Jayavarman was succeeded by a series of Hindu kings who disapproved of Preah Khan's dedication to Buddhism. These Hindu monarchs ordered that images of the Buddha should be cut away or transformed into carvings of Hindu ascetics – the tragic results of this early iconoclasm are all too visible today.

Preah Khan is simply vast. The site covers around 57 ha (140 acres). A laterite wall more than 2km (1¼ miles) long surrounds the whole complex, with carved *garuda* figures facing outwards every 50m (55yd). Access to the central sanctuary is by any one of four massive cross-shaped *gopura*, each located at one of the cardinal points of the compass. The best way to enter the temple is through the eastern gateway, though most taxi drivers will try to drop you at the west gate and collect you from the northern one. As with Angkor Thom, the causeways leading to the various gates are lined with gods to the left and demons to the right pulling the body of a serpent to churn the primordial ocean of milk in their 1,000-year search for the elixir of immortality.

1½km (1 mile) northeast from Angkor Thom's North Gate.

THE WHITE LADY SHRINE

The central sanctuary of Preah Khan is cruciform, with four entranceways. To the west of the east *gopura* lies the Hall of Dancers, named for the finely carved *apsara* images that line the walls. If the visitor is fit and agile enough to clamber over the great piles of fallen stone in the northeastern section of the main sanctuary, it is worth visiting the atmospheric 'Shrine of the White Lady', an elegant figure, supposedly not of an *apsara* but of a wife of King Jayavarman VII, concealed in a hidden room. The shrine is still venerated, and Cambodian supplicants light incense and candles, as well as leaving small offerings of money.

From 'Land Chen La' back to 'Water Chen La'

Following the reign of Indravarman III (1295–1308), the Kingdom of Angkor entered a period of slow but terminal decline. Between about 1350 and 1550, Cambodia's political and economic centre of gravity shifted inexorably back from 'Land Chen La' – that is, the Roluos–Angkor region at the head of the Tonlé Sap – to 'Water Chen La', the region around Phnom Penh, Lovek and Udong.

Some historians argue that this removal was due to the rise of the Thai Kingdom of Ayutthaya to the west and north of Angkor; others contend that the shift back to the southeast was also linked to the expansion of maritime trade between China and Southeast Asia which took place during the same period, making a move back towards the sea economically appealing. More than a dozen tributary missions were sent from Cambodia to China between 1371 and 1419, which is more than during the entire Angkor Period.

The rise of Thailand was certainly an important factor in the equation. The Thais, though once a tributary people who had served as mercenaries in the Khmer army, grew rapidly in number and in power. The threat to Cambodia became clear in 1350, with the foundation of the Thai Kingdom of Ayutthaya in the lower Chaophraya Basin, within easy striking distance of Angkor. War soon broke out, with the Thais generally gaining the upper hand. Angkor was captured and sacked on several occasions, most seriously in 1431.

In sparsely populated Southeast Asia, population was of more importance than land, and repeated Thai victories would have involved the large-scale transfer of defeated Cambodians to the west, depriving Angkor of the labour necessary for the maintenance of its great irrigation systems, as well as skilled stonemasons and other temple builders. As the Angkor region came under repeated Thai attack, 'Water Chen La' and the growing maritime trade with China became increasingly attractive as an alternative to an endless cycle of war, temple-building and intensive rice cultivation.

It seems probable that, while part of Angkor's population departed west as prisoners of the Thais, another part migrated southeast, to the vicinity of

Phnom Penh, in search of a more prosperous and secure existence. Significantly, this latter group would probably have included many of Angkor's richest and better educated classes – clerks, merchants, overseas businessmen, and perhaps private slave-owners and landholders.

But why choose the Phnom Penh region for a new capital? In fact, reasons were both plentiful and logical. To begin with, there seems to have been the well-established tradition of royal rule from the lower Mekong region dating back to 'Water Chen La' and Funan. It is also possible that the former royal region resented being ruled by Angkor, and that local chiefs were keen to trade directly with China on their own behalf.

Beyond this, there was the question of geographical location. Far from Ayutthaya and therefore safe from Thai attack, the Phnom Penh region was centred on the confluence of the Mekong, Sap and Bassac Rivers, and ideally placed for trade. The final move from Angkor seems to have taken place some time around 1440. From this time successive Cambodian administrations were established at Lovek and Udong and eventually Phnom Penh, the current capital.

A colourful shrine at Udong

Srah Srang and Banteay Kdei

West of Pre Rup the road heads due west past the great reservoir of Srah Srang, or 'Royal Bath'. This large body of water, 350m by 700m (1,148ft by 2,297ft), was built on the orders of Jayavarman V during the 10th century. A contemporaneous inscription records that 'water is stored here for the benefit of all creatures' – except, apparently, wild elephants, which the inscription denigrates as 'dyke breakers'. At the western side of the lake is a sandstone landing stage flanked by two lions and with balustrades bearing a large *garuda* on the back of a three-headed serpent. Srah Srang is a good spot to visit in the early morning when the rising sun illuminates the landing; it also makes a

ANGELINA JOLIE

Ta Prohm, Angkor's celebrated 'jungle temple', achieved widespread international recognition after the release of the popular film *Tomb Raider*, starring Angelina Jolie, in 2001. Both Angkor Wat and Ta Prohm figure prominently in the movie, with Jolie's character paddling a small canoe across the north tank in front of Angkor Wat, the temple's five towers reflected in its lotus-studded surface. Later she confronts and destroys a huge six-armed statue at Ta Prohm, with the director taking full advantage of the temple's eerie appeal. Today guides at Ta Prohm will happily point out the 'tomb raider tree' to visitors.

delightful sight in the late afternoon and early evening as water buffalo cool off in its tranquil shallows and small groups of Khmer children use the landing to dive into the waters.

Immediately behind the landing stage, a short distance further to the west, is a *gopura* in a tall laterite wall giving access to Banteay Kdei, the 'Citadel of the Cells'. Constructed on the orders of the master builder Jayavarman VII in the late 12th and early 13th centuries, it was established as a Buddhist temple in the Bayon style, similar in plan to Preah Khan and Ta Prohm, but less complex and smaller than either. Its structures are contained within two successive enclosure walls, and consist of two concentric galleries from which emerge towers, preceded to the east by a cloister. Banteay Kdei continued to function as a Buddhist monastic complex, on and off, until the mid-20th century. As a consequence of

Banteay Kdei, Angkor

Ta Keo, Angkor

this recent use, it is less overgrown than some of the other outer temples, and very pleasant to stroll through. Visitors are advised to follow the central corridor through the 'Hall of the Dancing Girls' – so called because of a bas-relief of dancers cut into the wall – and on to the central sanctuary which contains a relatively modern Buddha image, much venerated by the local people. At the western end of the complex a spectacular strangling fig tree enfolds part of the temple wall. *6½km (4 miles) east of Angkor Wat.*

Ta Keo and Thommanon

Located on the western edge of the great Eastern Baray, on the left bank of the Siem Reap River, Ta Keo is a massive temple mountain in the style of Bakheng and Pre Rup constructed by Jayavarman V and his successor, Surayavarman I, in the late 10th and early 11th centuries.

Built in the Khleang style, it was dedicated to the Hindu god Shiva in 1000 but never fully completed for reasons unknown. Enclosed by two walls, the temple has something of the stepped quality of a Babylonian ziggurat. The upper level, bearing five massive stone towers, is reached by four stairways ascending from the cardinal directions. At the foot of the east stairway is a fine carving of a kneeling Nandi, the bull mount of Shiva.

Just north and west of Ta Keo stands Spean Thma, a sandstone bridge dating from the Angkor era that still spans the narrow Siem Reap River. On the west side of the river, across from Ta Keo and close by Angkor Thom's Victory Gate, stands Thommanon, an early 12th-century Hindu temple dating from the reign of Surayavarman II. This small but impressive structure is notable for its fine carvings of female

Cattle wander through the grounds of Ta Prohm, Angkor

divinities. From here Angkor Thom may be entered via the Victory Gate.
Ta Keo is 1km (²/₃ miles) to the east of Angkor Thom's Victory Gate.
Thommanon is 250m (275yd) east of Victory Gate.

Ta Prohm

The truly spectacular temple of Ta Prohm or 'Ancestor of Brahma' is perhaps the most celebrated temple complex in Cambodia after Angkor Wat itself. This massive temple was, once again, the work of the indefatigable Jayavarman VII and dedicated to Buddhism. A stone stele, now safely preserved at the Angkor Conservatory, provides considerable detailed information concerning Ta Prohm. From this unique source we know that, in its prime, Ta Prohm owned 3,140 villages and was maintained by 79,365 people including 18 high priests, 2,740 officials, 2,202 assistants and 615 dancers. Other statistics recorded for posterity and no doubt intended to emphasise the magnificence of the temple as well as the wealth, power and munificence of its founder, Jayavarman VII, record that Ta Prohm owned a set of gold dishes weighing more than 500kg (1,100lb), 35 diamonds, 40,620 pearls, 876 Chinese veils, 512 silk beds and 523 parasols. Needless to add, all this treasure has long since disappeared.

Ta Prohm is a long, low complex of buildings all standing at the same level. A series of concentric galleries are connected by passages that provide welcome shade in the heat of the day. The entire complex is surrounded by a rectangular laterite wall around 700m by 1,000m (2,300ft by 3,280ft) long. The temple is best entered from the east by a magnificent but semi-collapsed *gopura*, now filled with damaged Buddha images possibly awaiting restoration. Beyond this is a sandstone building with finely carved false doorways known as the 'Hall of the Dancers'. This structure, easily identified by its square pillars, is thought to have been used for the performance of religious or ritual dance, in symbolism of which the walls are decorated with rows of graceful *apsara*.

The central sanctuary is readily identifiable by the simplicity of its stone surfacing, which was never carved. Experts postulate that it may formerly have been decorated with stucco and gilding which has crumbled away or been removed over the years. Elsewhere there are many finely carved details, especially the delicately incised *apsara* and the elaborate *gopura*.

But what makes Ta Prohm both unique and the favourite of so many visitors to Angkor is that, following a courageous and pioneering archaeological decision, the jungle has only been partially cut back, leaving the towers and cloisters covered with the roots of huge strangling fig, banyan and kapok trees which rise high above the temple. Spectacular roots like giant melted Gruyère cheese bind lintels and crack vaulted passageways, whilst birds flit from tree to tree in the upper canopy, breaking the stillness with their shrill cries. At Ta Prohm it is easy to imagine the sense of awe that Henri Mouhot and other early European explorers of Angkor must have felt, for this truly seems a lost 'jungle temple', symbolic of Angkor's glorious past and of centuries of abandonment.

2km (1¼ miles) southeast of Angkor Thom's Victory Gate.

Angkor

A giant tree's roots spread over a wall at Ta Prohm, Angkor

Roluos and beyond

Beyond Angkor's Grand Circuit, but within the historical and cultural context of the Angkor region, are numerous significant sites and relics. The most important are now easily visited and include the Roluos Group, which predate Angkor itself and date back to the 9th century, the exquisite gem-like temple of Banteay Srei, and the mysterious and evocative Kbal Spean, Angkor's 'River of a Thousand Linga'.

Banteay Srei

Banteay Srei, whose name means 'Citadel of Women', is widely considered – together with Angkor Wat, the Bayon and Ta Prohm – to be one of the jewels of Cambodian historical monuments. A finely executed miniature temple in pink and roseate sandstone, Banteay Srei was dedicated in 967, the only major temple in the Angkor region not built by monarchy. According to the founding stele, which was discovered by a French archaeologist in 1936, it was established by a Hindu priest named Yajnyavahara, who served as a counsellor to King Rajendravarman. According to the stele (which, one must assume, Yajnyavahara paid for), he was a scholar and a philanthropist who helped those who suffered from illness, injustice or poverty. Be this as it may, he certainly left a magnificent monument for posterity.

Banteay Srei is of rectangular design, enclosed by three walls and the remains of a moat. The visitor should enter by the main entrance on the east side, through a cruciform laterite gateway decorated with a carving of Indra on a three-headed elephant. This is followed by a processional way that runs for around 80m (260ft) between pink sandstone pillars, then another gateway carved with a scene showing Sita abducted by the demon-king Ravana.

The central complex comprises a number of structures including, most importantly, shrines dedicated to Shiva (the central and southern buildings) and to Vishnu (the northern building). The shrines are guarded by beautifully carved figures, most sadly damaged. Some of the best figures have been taken away for safekeeping to Phnom Penh. Some side panels, too, have disappeared and been replaced by crude, uncarved laterite. The originals are held at the Musée Guimet in Paris.

Apsara, Banteay Srei, near Angkor

The themes represented in the carved lintels and frontons are derived from the Hindu epic *Ramayana*, and include representations of Shiva, Parvati, Hanuman, Krishna and the evil Ravana, a figure easily distinguished by his demonic visage, and multiple heads and arms. Also remarkable are the finely carved figures of male and female divinities set in niches in the central towers. The style, classified by art historians as 'Banteay Srei style', represents female divinities with plaits or buns, wearing loosely draped skirts or sarongs. They wear heavy and elaborate jewellery at their ears, necks, waists, arms and ankles. The male divinities carry spears and wear loincloths.

Banteay Srei lies about 30km (18½ miles) from Siem Reap via a road running northeast from the 'Grand Circuit' between Pre Rup and the East Mebon. Open: daily 5am–5pm.

The Roluos Group

The small town of Roluos, about 13km (8 miles) southeast of Siem Reap, lies near the 'Roluos Group' which includes the earliest temple monuments to have been built in the Angkor region. About 11 centuries ago King Jayavarman II (802–50), the founder of the Khmer Empire, established his capital at Hariharalaya, approximately on the site of today's Roluos Township.

Within 3km (2 miles), there survive three important complexes. To the north of National Highway 6, the main

Spirit house at Bakong, near Angkor

Siem Reap–Phnom Penh road, stands the ancient temple of Lolei, whilst to the south may be found the larger temples of Preah Ko and Bakong.

Bakong is a massive late 9th-century Hindu temple dedicated to the god Shiva. Today the site is also home to an active contemporary Buddhist temple. More than 1,000 years ago Bakong was the central feature of Jayavarman II's capital of Hariharalaya. It was constructed as a temple mountain on an artificial mound surrounded by a moat and outer enclosure walls. By far the largest monument of the Roluos Group, it should be entered from the east along a raised causeway decorated with seven-headed *naga* serpents. Long covered buildings on each side of the main eastern *gopura* are thought to have served as rest houses for pilgrims visiting the shrine. In the northeastern and southeastern corners of the complex stand four buildings with vents which may have served as crematoriums.

The central part of Bakong rests on the artificial mound representing Mount Meru. This mound is surrounded by eight large brick towers which retain some fine examples of decoration in carved sandstone. The square mound, which appears like a stepped pyramid in design, rises behind these towers in five stages, the first three of which have stone elephants at the corners. At the summit is the central sanctuary which is square, with four levels and a lotus-shaped tower in the middle. It is believed that this lotus finial was constructed at a later date, possibly having been added to Bakong in the 12th century.

Established by King Yasovarman I (889–910), **Lolei** was dedicated to the Hindu deity Shiva. Its style is considered transitional between the nearby monuments of Bakong and Preah Ko. Lolei is best known for its fine carvings and well-preserved stone inscriptions, though the four central brick towers have partly collapsed and are covered with undergrowth. The temple is based on a double platform rising from a reservoir – generally dry except during the rainy season – and surrounded by a laterite wall. Stone

lions guard the stairways leading to the main temple. The best-preserved inscriptions are carved into the lintels and side posts of the temple's false doors. They are in such fine condition that they appear almost new. Only the crumbling stone at the edge of the false doorways suggests that they are more than a millennium old.

Built by King Indravarman I (877–89), **Preah Ko**, the 'Sacred Bull', is a Hindu temple dedicated to the worship of Shiva, constructed in memory of Indravarman's parents and that of Jayavarman II, the founder of the Khmer Empire.

Preah Ko is in an attractive rural setting and, being some distance from the main Angkor circuit, is tranquil and rarely visited. The walls and gateways of the outer enclosure have largely collapsed, but the inner enclosure is in much better shape. Some restoration has taken place over the last decade. Approaching the central area from the east, the remains of three statues of Nandi, the sacred bull and mount of Shiva after whom the temple is named, may be seen.

The main sanctuary of Preah Ko consists of six brick towers set on a low laterite platform. Formerly each tower would have contained the image of a Hindu deity, but these have long disappeared. The quality of the carved decorative motifs on the false doors, lintels and columns is magnificent. The carving on the east towers perhaps surpasses that on the west. Notable themes include *kala*, monstrous creatures with bulging eyes, a lion's snout, horns, clawed hands and leering mouths; *makara*, huge sea animals with reptilian bodies and elongated trunk-like snouts; and *garuda*, winged creatures with thick beaks and sharp claws that serve as Vishnu's flying mount.

For Bakong, turn right off National Highway 6 approximately 12km (7½ miles) from Siem Reap and continue south for 1km (²/₃ mile).

For Lolei, turn left off National Highway 6. 150m (165yd) after the right turn to Preah Ko and Bakong. Continue north for about 300m (330yd).

For Preah Ko, turn right off National Highway 6 approximately 12km (7½ miles) from Siem Reap and continue south for 300m (330yd).

Stupas at Lolei, near Angkor

River of a Thousand Linga

Hidden in the mountains about 25km (16 miles) to the north of the main temple complexes at Angkor, Kbal Spean, which means 'Head Bridge' in Khmer, has only been safe to visit for about a decade. More commonly known as the 'River of a Thousand Linga', it can only be reached by a fairly steep climb of about 3km (2 miles) from the road below running between Siem Reap and the more northerly town of Anlong Veng.

Kbal Spean is remarkable for a series of carvings cut into the living stone in, around and beneath the waters of the Kbal Spean River. There are three prominent themes or motifs, including *linga* or stylised male sexual organs used as a symbol for the worship of the Hindu deity Shiva; *yoni* or stylised female sexual organs often associated with the Hindu goddess Shakti, and generally coupled, for obvious reasons, with the Shiva *lingam*; and representations of Hindu deities and associated animals, notably of Shiva himself.

Most of Kbal Spean's archaeological vestiges have been dated to the 11th, 12th and 13th centuries. The founder of the 'River of a Thousand Linga' was Surayavarman I (1002–49), and

the process was largely completed by Udayadiyavarman II (1050–66). Their purpose was to symbolically fertilise the waters flowing from the Kulen Mountains, via the Kbal Spean–Siem Reap River, to the great *baray* reservoirs of Angkor and the rice fields of the Khmer kingdom.

Kbal Spean itself is a natural stone bridge which has given its name to the river it crosses as well as to the sacred site established along the river more than 1,000 years ago. From just upstream of the natural bridge to the north, down as far as the waterfall below, the Kbal Spean river bed is covered with a plethora of carved *linga*, symbolising the god Shiva's supreme essence. Some of the *linga* appear to rest on pedestals in the form of their female counterpart, *yoni*.

The stone banks of the river, as well as basins carved deep into the stone of the river bed, are similarly sculpted with Hindu scenes, symbols and inscriptions. These include the god Vishnu reclining in meditation with a lotus flower growing from his navel. The god Brahma sits on the bud of the lotus. The flow of the Kbal Spean River constantly washes over these representations, becoming lustral water in the process, before dividing into the Siem Reap and Puok Rivers to fertilise the rice plains below, then passing into the great lake of Tonlé Sap.

The trail to Kbal Spean is well marked, leading through secondary jungle and across small streams which are crossed by simple wooden bridges. Where the trail is steep, steps have been cut into the hill. It's possible to visit alone, but it may be best to hire the services of a guide at a travel agency in Siem Reap. The waterfall is at its best at the end of the rainy season in September and October.

35km (22 miles) north of Siem Reap.

Semi-submerged *linga* and *yoni* at the 'River of a Thousand Linga', Kbal Spean

Getting away from it all

Cambodia should be a wonderful destination for seclusion seekers. It has pristine beaches, tropical rivers and lakes, unspoiled and all but unvisited mountain ranges and beautiful, fertile lowlands. Unfortunately, three decades of war devastated the national infrastructure and left huge areas of land littered with deadly, concealed land mines. All that is now changing fast, and every year new areas, many rarely or not at all visited by travellers in times past, are opening up.

Enjoying nature

It's a sad fact that not only people suffered during the long years of destructive warfare that plagued Cambodia for much of almost six decades between 1941 and 1998. Wildlife was bombed and blown up by mines, killed for food – or, by young Khmer Rouge soldiers, even for fun – and deforestation was (and remains) widespread. But things are improving, not least as locals realise that rare and endangered species are worth more alive as tourist attractions, than dead as food – or aphrodisiacs.

Dolphin watching at Kratie

The little river port of Kratie in the far northeast is well off the beaten track. Known chiefly for its fine but dilapidated colonial architecture, the town's main attraction is now dolphin watching.

A nearby stretch of the Mekong River is home to a group of rare Irrawaddy dolphins; the Mekong Dolphin Conservation Project estimates that there are only about 170 of these intelligent and delightful creatures left in the upper stretches of the Cambodian Mekong. In nearby Myanmar (Burma), where they are also endangered, Irrawaddy dolphins have been observed helping humans to fish, using acoustic signals to drive fish into nets. Cambodian fishermen say that they never deliberately catch dolphins for food, but now that the tourist appeal of these charming creatures is apparent, they are much more careful to avoid killing or otherwise disturbing them (*see also pp48–9*).

348km (216 miles) from Phnom Penh on National Highway 7. Two air-con buses leave at 7.30am and take six hours. Share taxis take four to six hours.

Flooded forests and floating villages

Cambodia is a fortunate and fertile land, where – were it not for the foolishness of man – there should never be a famine. The source and origin of this amazing fertility, enabling the growth of as many as three rice crops a year and an apparently endless supply of fish, are the many rivers and, more especially, the great central lake. Tonlé Sap is like nothing else in this world, a freshwater lake that shrinks and expands by up to three times according to season. It is home to an amazing variety of wildlife, as well as local fisherfolk who live in stilt houses and floating villages. A boat journey through the flooded forests of Tonlé Sap can be a magical experience (*see also p79*).

Prek Toal Biosphere

If you have spent several days exploring Angkor and find yourself suffering from 'temple fatigue', or if you just want to get away from the increasing numbers of tourists visiting these fantastic temple complexes, Prek Toal Biosphere on the northwestern shore of Tonlé Sap might be just the solution. Billed as the premier bird-watching destination in all Southeast Asia, it is home to a plethora of rare and large water birds such as stork, ibis, crane and pelican, without a single tour bus for miles (*see also pp80–81*).

From Siem Reap it's 12km (7½ miles) to the port of Chong Kneas, then 18km (11 miles) by boat from Chong Kneas.

Scenic coasts

Half a century ago, Cambodia's coastline was viewed by the French colonial authorities as Indochina's Riviera. Like the rest of the country, it suffered terribly during the long years of war, but it is now making a remarkable comeback.

Betel and coconut palm on the edge of one of Cambodia's many forests

Diving and water sports

Sihanoukville (*see pp67–9*) is the country's main port and seaside resort, with four main beaches offering fine swimming and sunbathing, as well as all manner of water sports, both near the shore, and on neighbouring islands which can be reached by water taxi for diving, snorkelling and game fishing. Other less developed destinations are Kep to the east near the Vietnamese border (*see pp66–7*) and Koh Kong to the west, on the border with Thailand.

Islands off the beaten track

Cambodia has many islands (*koh* in Khmer) off its southern coast in the warm waters of the Gulf of Thailand. The islands of Kompong Som lie to the west of Sihanoukville within a half-day boat trip. The group of islands known as Koh Ream are scattered to the east towards the fishing village of Phsar Ream. Koh Tang is further out to sea, between four and eight hours' journey from Sihanoukville by boat.

Local dive companies recommend the Kompong Som group, especially Koh Koang Kang and Koh Rong Samloem, for swimming and snorkelling during the hot and rainy seasons (March to October). Koh Rong Samloem has a beautiful strand of beach on its southwest side, stretching for about 5km (3 miles). It has fresh water resources on the island and a bustling fishing community in the southeast with basic supplies including fresh water, shrimp, crab and fish.

Koh Ream, which is more protected by the mainland, is a better bet during the cool season (November to

Coconut palms abound along the coast and on the offshore islands

February) when the winds blow from the north. For snorkelling, the waters around Koh Chraloh, Koh Ta Kiev and Koh Khteah are recommended, though the proximity of the mainland and related higher levels of silt can reduce visibility, especially in choppy weather. Finally Koh Tang and the nearby islands are popular with more experienced divers who may wish to spend a night or two away from the mainland, either moored in the lee of one of the islands or camping on shore. This whole area is rich in a diverse marine life, with large fish, excellent visibility and sunken wrecks to explore.

There are also numerous islands off Kep, including popular Koh Tonsay, also known as 'Rabbit Island', which can easily be reached by boat and makes a popular excursion. The island has four small beaches with good swimming and snorkelling (*see pp66–7*).

Further out to sea, on the ferry route between Sihanoukville and Koh Kong, Koh Sdach is the most important of the tiny and remote Samit Islands, where the adventurous traveller may stay overnight. The beach is more pebbles than sand, but the snorkelling and fishing is good, and the island has a few simple guesthouses and restaurants.

National parks

Cambodia's first national parks were established as recently as 1993. Today there are seven national parks, Kirirom, Phnom Bokor, Kep, Ream, Botum Sakor, Phnom Kulen and Virachey.

Giant ferns at Virachay National Park

There are also ten designated wildlife sanctuaries at Mount Aural, Peam Krasop and Phnom Samkos (all in Koh Kong), Roniem Daun Sam in Battambang, Kulen Prom Tep in Siem Reap-Preah Vihear, Boung Per in Kampong Thom, Lumphat in Ratanakiri-Mondulkiri, Phnom Prich in Mondulkiri-Kratie, Phnom Nam Lyr in Mondulkiri, and finally Snoul in Kratie.

The most accessible and popular national parks are Phnom Bokor, Kirirom and Ream. Virachey is much more remote, but offers perhaps the best opportunities in the country for 'getting away from it all', seeing minority peoples and rare wildlife, boating and trekking on reasonably priced and professionally organised tours.

Small stream in Kirirom National Park

Bokor National Park

The old French period hill station of Bokor (*see p65*) is the gateway to Bokor National Park. With an area of 1,400sq km (540sq miles) spanning four southern provinces in the Cardamom Mountains, the park contains a unique range of habitats and supports a rich diversity of flora and fauna. *35km (22 miles) west of Kampot off National Highway 3 on the road to Sihanoukville.*

Kirirom National Park

Cambodia's first national park, Kirirom lies on the eastern edge of the Dâmrei Mountains at an average height of 675m (2,215ft) above sea level. Noted for its pine trees and orchids, it has many hiking trails and footpaths leading to small lakes and waterfalls. *112km (70 miles) southwest of Phnom Penh off National Highway 4 on the road to Sihanoukville.*
Park HQ Tel: (023) 214 409. Open: daily 8.30am–6pm. Admission charge.

Ream National Park

A convenient day trip from Sihanoukville, Ream National Park encompasses 150sq km (56sq miles) of land habitat and a further 60sq km

(23sq miles) of marine habitat, with beaches, mangrove forest and tropical jungle. It is home to 150 bird species and a large monkey population.

By the coast 18km (11 miles) southeast of Sihanoukville off National Highway 4. Park HQ Tel: (012) 875 096. Open: daily 8.30am–6pm. Admission charge.

Virachey National Park

Lying along the southern frontier of Laos and the western frontier of Vietnam, Virachey National Park is truly remote, and includes the '*naga*'s tail' area in the country's far northeast. Fauna includes slow loris, pygmy loris, pig-tailed macaque, long-tailed macaque, douc langur and yellow-cheeked crested gibbon, as well as elephant, tiger, gaur and bintang. The area is also home to some of Cambodia's smallest and least known minorities, including the Kreung, Kavet, Brao and Lun peoples. Despite its extreme remoteness, Virachey is one of Cambodia's best administered national parks, offering short, medium and long tours from the park HQ at Banlung, the capital of Ratanakiri Province.

Ratanakiri Province. Tel: (075) 974 176. www.bpamp.org.kh. Open: daily 8.30am–6pm. Admission charge. Currently there are no flights between Phnom Penh and Banlung. An air-con bus leaves daily from Phnom Penh at 7am and arrives in Stung Treng at 5pm. From Stung Treng hire a taxi for the 165km (103 mile) trip to Banlung.

Getting away from it all

Colourful vegetation at Virachey National Park

When to go

Cambodia, like the majority of mainland Southeast Asia, has three main seasons. The rainy season, marked by the coming of the monsoon between May and July, can last until as late as November. During this period, the weather is hot, humid and wet. The monsoon is followed by a cool, dry phase, from November until mid-February. The third season, hot and dry, begins in late February and lasts until May.

Between May and October, the southwest monsoon brings daily rainfall, with rain normally falling heavily for a few hours in the late afternoons. The wettest months are usually September and October. This can be a good time to visit if you don't intend getting off the beaten track. In more remote areas roads can turn to mud and become impassable. The temples at Angkor can be relatively free of visitors and the southern beaches almost deserted. By the end of this period the countryside blooms, and the lush, almost fluorescent green rice fields make a wonderful picture. Rivers and streams are replenished and the cycle of life continues.

Cooler temperatures arrive with the northwest monsoon between November and March and rainfall dwindles. This is certainly the best

Sugar palms and rice paddy, central Cambodia

season to visit Cambodia and consequently Angkor can get very busy. Sihanoukville and the offshore islands make a welcoming retreat. The coolest months are between November and January, though even then temperatures rarely fall below 20°C (68°F). Just occasionally a cold snap hits the country, usually from the north, and temperatures can go below this typical minimum. But it is certainly not an annual occurrence. The driest months are January and February, when there is little or no rainfall.

The hot season, late February to May, can be quite unpleasant, especially April, when temperatures can go over 40°C (104°F). It's not a good time to visit.

Rainfall can vary quite significantly from year to year and region to region. The Cardamom and Elephant mountain ranges block the natural flow

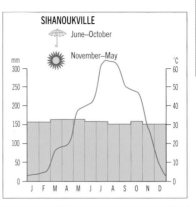

SIHANOUKVILLE
June–October
November–May

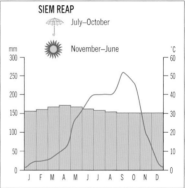

SIEM REAP
July–October
November–June

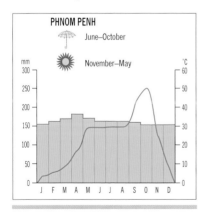

PHNOM PENH
June–October
November–May

WEATHER CONVERSION CHART

25.4mm = 1 inch
°F = 1.8 × °C + 32

of the southwest monsoon towards the central plains and consequently this area is prone to droughts. This can cause severe food shortages for the many Cambodians dependent on the Tonlé Sap and its surrounding fertile soils for their sustenance. The central plains commonly average only 1,400mm (55in), while the southwestern highlands, with their seaward-facing inclines, can exceed 5,500mm (217in) a year. The country's coast also receives some heavy annual rainfall; Sihanoukville as much as 5,000mm (197in).

Getting around

Transportation in Cambodia and the infrastructure which supports it has improved over the past few years, but quite frankly that was not difficult as travelling around Cambodia even just five years ago could be very trying. Improved roads mean that travelling times by car or bus have been cut dramatically on the major routes. The country's river system used to be an attractive alternative to its roads, but these days fewer visitors choose this form of transportation.

By air

By far the quickest way to get from Phnom Penh to Siem Reap is by air. Siem Reap Airways flies both ways six times a day. At present this is the only domestic route in operation. Domestic airlines come and go in Cambodia as do the routes they fly, so it's best to check with your travel agent when planning your trip to see if any new routes have been added.

By bus

Bus transport has improved vastly over the last few years with many roads around the country being upgraded. Travelling times between Phnom Penh and the provinces have consequently also improved. Air-conditioned buses serve all the major tourist towns. The **Phnom Penh Sorya Transport Company** (*corner of streets 217 and 67. Tel: (023) 210 859. www. ppsoryatransport.com*) runs regular services to Ho Chi Minh City, Bangkok, Sihanoukville, Siem Reap, Battambang

and a number of other towns. **Mekong Express** (*87 Sisowath Quay, corner of 102 Street. Tel: (023) 427 518*) runs similar routes, but in slightly more luxurious buses.

There is no city bus service in Phnom Penh.

By train

Train travel in Cambodia is best avoided. The rolling stock is old, slow and uncomfortable. Trains to Sihanoukville and Kampot run every other day and the journey takes approximately six hours. Timings are random, but if a train leaves Phnom Penh on a Tuesday then it will return from Sihanoukville on a Wednesday. The other route runs to Battambang and also leaves Phnom Penh every other day. It takes 14 hours to get to and from Battambang.

By boat

With the huge improvement in road connections boats are no longer as popular with visitors as they were. The safety angle also now plays an important part in choosing between an air-conditioned bus and an overcrowded boat. Often boat operators sell far more tickets than there are seats aboard and passengers end up sitting on the roof. This is great for views, but not very safe. Nevertheless, travelling by boat does give a different perspective on the country. The most popular route, Phnom Penh to Siem Reap, travelling along the Sap River and then across the vast Tonlé Sap Lake, offers a real insight into the fishing communities along the way. The journey takes roughly five hours and costs approximately US$20. Boats for Siem Reap depart from the tourist boat dock on Sisowath Quay opposite Street 106 from around 7am. Another popular route is between Siem Reap and Battambang.

Boats no longer run between Phnom Penh and Kompong Cham due to the much improved road system around

Taxis can be hired at very reasonable rates

Getting around

the capital. From Kompong Cham, one boat a day leaves for Kratie, with a journey time of three hours. This boat continues beyond Kratie to Stung Treng in the north of the country.

A popular way of getting to Thailand involves taking a boat from Sihanoukville via Koh Kong, but be aware that the boats used are often river boats and are no match for storms at sea. The Gulf of Thailand can get quite rough at times.

By taxi and car hire

Taxis are available at both Phnom Penh and Siem Reap International airports, but don't expect to find metered ones. Most taxis in Phnom Penh are also unmarked, so the best way to arrange a taxi is either through a travel agent or your hotel. One reliable 24-hour operator is **Taxi Vantha** (*Tel: (012) 855 000. www.taxivantha.com*). Costs in and around Phnom Penh vary between US$2 and US$5 for a short trip to as much as US$35 for a day's hire.

In Siem Reap taxis are plentiful and are always ready and willing to take customers to the temples, preferring all-day rates to shorter trips. Daily rates are US$30, although it might be possible to negotiate a better rate if you expect to use the taxi for more than one day. Rates do rise if you wish to visit temples or other sights further

A boat tour across Tonlé Sap offers a unique perspective on Cambodia

away such as Kbal Spean or Banteay Srei.

Share taxis ply the routes between Phnom Penh and most major towns and can sometimes be a good option. Drivers often wait to fill the vehicle up, but once filled there are no stops, so this can be a quick way to reach your destination.

Motorcycle hire

It's possible to hire a motorcycle and drive all over Cambodia, although it's not necessarily recommended unless you are an experienced rider. Traffic in Phnom Penh can be chaotic and roads in the provinces vary from very good to downright awful. Typical rental charges go from US$5 per day for a 100cc bike, perfect for driving in the city, to US$10 per day for a larger 250cc machine. Remember to always wear a helmet, which is mandatory, even if the law is seldom enforced.

By motorcycle taxi

Seen all over the country, the *motodop*, regularly shortened to just *moto*, is the most common form of public transport. These motorcycle taxis can be found on every street corner. Drivers are usually identifiable by the hats they wear (few wear crash helmets) and the bikes themselves usually have larger seats than the average motorbike. For short distances the *moto* is often the best way to get around and in the tourist areas many drivers can speak some English. Journeys can cost as little

Cyclo driver and family, Phnom Penh

as 1,500 riel, although you might well pay more than this in Siem Reap. The golden rule: always agree a fare before getting going.

By *cyclo*

If you have plenty of time a *cyclo* or pedicab can be a great way of getting about and seeing the sights. *Cyclos* can be found on most streets and especially near markets in urban areas. Fares usually range from around 1,000 to 4,000 riel. Unfortunately, the *cyclo* is becoming quite a rare sight in some parts of the country, losing out to the ubiquitous *moto*.

Accommodation

When Cambodia first reopened to tourism more than a decade ago, accommodation in both Phnom Penh and Siem Reap was limited, poor and unattractive. Fortunately today, especially in Siem Reap, a new hotel seems to be going up every week.

Cambodian hotels present accommodation options to suit all budgets, but they are on the whole limited to a few tourist centres. Joint enterprises with some of the world's top hotel groups have led to the development of hotels in Phnom Penh and Siem Reap whose commitment to excellence is faultless. International chains such as InterContinental, Le Meridien, Raffles and Sofitel have all established properties of high standards, with prices to match.

Cambodia's top hotels tend to be either very modern and large, with all kinds of facilities such as business centre, gym and tennis courts, or former colonial mansions that are full of character and offer a more personalised service but fewer facilities. Most of these top-end places tend to be concentrated in Phnom Penh, Siem Reap and along the south coast. Some of the very best offer lavish spas, interior decoration by globally famous designers and haute cuisine.

Just below these five-star luxury properties lies the realm of the locally managed high-end hotels. These offer all the amenities and standards you would find at home, but without the sophisticated service of the international chains. A number of these hotels have sprung up in Siem

Hotel Cambodiana, Phnom Penh

Renakse Hotel, Phnom Penh

Reap over the last few years and still more are being planned. The hotel-building boom that has hit Siem Reap over the last few years has been staggering. Consequently, there are some great bargains to be had in this particular range.

The supply of mid-range options in tourist areas has also grown immeasurably over the last decade. These mid-range hotels are fine for a few nights, but don't expect luxury; they vary a lot in what they offer, so it's best to look first if you can. There is no clear distinction in Cambodia between hotels, guesthouses, lodges and inns, and some of the well-run guesthouses are better than cheap hotels.

Guesthouses can now be found all across the country, some in the most unlikely places. As in neighbouring Laos, and Thailand 20 years ago, these more unlikely venues tend to attract the intrepid backpacker. In the tourist heartlands of Phnom Penh, Siem Reap and Sihanoukville guesthouses abound, but unfortunately they are of greatly varying standards. Some are really quite excellent and offer a number of facilities; others are no more than flophouses. It's always best to check out the rooms before checking in, especially in Phnom Penh.

Sihanoukville and the coast have also seen something of a building boom over the last few years and it's now

Raffles Grand Hotel d'Angkor, Siem Reap

possible to find resorts that offer all-inclusive rates, with good children's facilities and a safe environment.

The islands off the south coast are just beginning to realise their potential, but at the moment accommodation is mostly limited to small family-run bungalow operations. It is likely that the larger hotel operators will use these islands to expand the tourism industry in Cambodia over the next few years, looking to Thailand to see what can be achieved.

The star rating system for hotels is generally reliable, but can be erratic at the lower end. Most rooms include a private bathroom, mosquito meshing on the windows and doors, plus a fan or air-conditioning. Many hotels have rooms at various prices, reflecting the facilities available or other aspects like size of room and view, so it's worth checking out a few before you decide.

As with most destinations, price reflects quality, and rates vary from just a few dollars for a small, windowless room to hundreds of dollars for a penthouse suite with a glorious view. As a rule, all hotels in Cambodia quote their prices in US dollars, as do most small guesthouses, although you may find a few in the more remote provinces quoting in riel.

Prices can vary according to the season. High season is from mid-November to February. During this period, it is advisable to have a prior booking, which is easily done by visiting one of the many websites dedicated to hotel bookings such as www.asiahotels.com or www.cambodia-hotels.com or visiting the websites quoted in the listings in the Directory section (pp158–73). Prices in those listings are generally for the high season. If you are travelling during the low season, you may be able to negotiate a discount of up to 30 per cent, depending on your bargaining ability.

Not all hotels of the mid-range and below categories will accept credit cards, so always enquire in advance. Check-out time is usually at noon, and half-day rates are often charged if you wish to stay a few hours longer.

If you're not coming on a pre-booked tour, accommodation information (as well as many touts) will be waiting for you at the airport. It's easier, and often considerably cheaper, to book online – and most places, even down to quite modest guesthouses, will send a car to meet guests at the airport.

All top-end hotels offer internet facilities as do many mid-range establishments. Some guesthouses in the tourist areas double as internet cafés. Most hotels and guesthouses offering rooms above the US$20 mark will be air-conditioned and usually have cable or satellite television, refrigerator and facilities for making tea and coffee.

Tap water is not generally safe to drink in any hotel or guesthouse. Luxury and mid-range level hotels will always provide mini-bars with drinking water as well as soft drinks and beer.

When travelling off the beaten track remember that accommodation is limited and it's a good idea to arrive before sundown to give yourself a chance to actually find something. If you are really stuck it's best to ask at the local police station where they ought to be able to help out. If all else fails head for the nearest temple and ask the abbot for his permission to stay. He'll be surprised, but will usually find somewhere for the visitor to rest. Always leave a donation on leaving the following morning.

Most top-class hotels have outdoor swimming pools

Food and drink

Cambodia has always been a fertile land, rich in rice, fish, vegetables and fruit; just like in neighbouring Thailand, nobody should ever go hungry. Tragically, in the late 20th century more than a million people starved to death as a direct result of Khmer Rouge policies and an indirect result of administrative incompetence. In the period between 1975 and 1978 almost nobody in Cambodia, apart from the Khmer Rouge leadership, had enough to eat.

It is unfortunately impossible to keep the Khmer Rouge out of contemporary matters, even if the subject is food and drink. Virtually everyone in this dreadful period was malnourished to the point of starvation. Rice was scarce in this rice-rich land because the KR was exporting it to China and North Korea in exchange for weapons. Cambodians have never forgotten these years and consequently they are infatuated by food. These days there's plenty to eat and the quality of ingredients is improving all the time, as are the standards of the restaurants.

Khmer cuisine is often likened to Thai food, but without the intense spiciness. This view does have some accuracy and for some visitors it is actually a boon. Other major influences include China and Vietnam, but the French left a legacy of bread, and consequently Cambodians eat a lot more bread than any of their neighbours.

The country's main staple is rice, with which almost all meals are accompanied. The extensive river system and the giant Tonlé Sap provide abundant freshwater fish and prawns in addition to which plenty of fresh seafood is obtainable from the Gulf of Thailand.

Meat and poultry are widely available from the markets, but are generally more expensive than the freshwater fish from the rivers and lakes. In the countryside, other less well known local delicacies include land crabs, field rats, locusts and snakes. In the town of Skuon, between Phnom Penh and Kompong Cham, the local villagers specialise in huge, deep-fried spiders, which they sell to any passing bus passenger or lorry driver.

Being a tropical country, Cambodia has a wealth of fruit. Much of it is seasonal and, particularly towards the end of the hot season, the markets are filled with a wide variety of exotic fruits. Some of the more popular ones include coconut, durian, jackfruit, mango, mangosteen, pineapple, rambutan, watermelon and a surprisingly wide variety of bananas.

Upcountry food choices are generally limited to Cambodian fare or to the ever-present baguette and pâté. Chinese food is commonly available in provincial capitals due to the number of overseas Chinese migrants found in these centres. Thai cuisine is widespread in the western areas of the country, especially Battambang and Siem Reap where there are numerous Thai restaurants. In the east, Vietnamese culinary influence is strong. Down on the coast, and especially in Sihanoukville, seafood is popular and is cooked in every conceivable way.

As is to be expected of a capital city, Phnom Penh has the most extensive choice of restaurants in the country. Here the visitor can find all the styles listed above as well as French, Greek, Indian, Italian, Malay and Turkish restaurants. In fact Phnom Penh serves some of the best French food available in Southeast Asia.

Similarly Siem Reap, with its huge influx of visitors over the last few years, has been transformed into something of a gourmet's paradise. With fine Thai restaurants and a bewildering array of world food around town, nobody should go hungry. Even the low-end guesthouses frequently have good kitchens and the luxury hotels, particularly the Raffles Grand Hotel d'Angkor, serve some of the finest dishes on the planet.

Food and drink

Crispy rice and curry, typical Cambodian cuisine

Food and drink

Food vendor, Sisowath Quay, Phnom Penh

The concept of Western-style vegetarianism is alien to most Cambodians even though they are Buddhists. Most believe that if you can afford meat or fish then you should eat it as it will obviously improve any meal. Travelling in Cambodia can therefore be a trial for vegetarians and vegans. Stir-fried vegetable dishes and rice and vegetable combinations can be produced, but the likelihood of these being cooked in separate pans from the other meat dishes is small. In the tourist areas many of the better restaurants will have a vegetarian section on their menus.

A typical Khmer meal will usually consist of a soup (*somla*), a fish or meat dish and a salad. Popular soup dishes include *somla chapek* (pork and ginger soup), *somla machou bangkang* (sour and spicy prawn soup), *somla machou banle* (sour fish soup) and *moan sngor* (coriander and chicken soup). A regular fish dish might be *dt'ray aing* (grilled fish) which can be found just about everywhere, *dt'ray chean neung spey* (fried fish with vegetables) or *dt'ray aing k'nyei* (grilled catfish with ginger sauce). Meat dishes such as *saich moan chha khnhei* (stir-fried chicken with ginger) or *saich koh aing* (grilled beef) are popular. Cambodian salads are quite different from their Western counterparts and are usually very spicy. A typical example might be *phlea saich koh* (grilled beef, coriander and mint salad). Essential condiments to accompany any Cambodian meal are *prahoc* (fish sauce) and *tuk dt'ray* (fish sauce with ground, roasted peanuts). Fish and meat dishes not served with rice are generally accompanied by noodles.

Some other popular Khmer dishes include *hamok* (fish with coconut milk steamed in a banana leaf), *moan dhomrei* (sliced chicken sautéed with holy basil), *somla machou saich koh* (sour beef stew), *choeeng chomni jruk chean* (fried pork spare ribs), *cha'ung cha'ni jruk ang* (spare ribs marinated with mushrooms) and *khao poun* (rice noodles in a coconut sauce). A particularly delicious, but rich dish, *an sam jruk* (pork and soybeans marinated in ginger and chilli), is also popular throughout the country.

Soft drinks and beer are available everywhere. All the major international soft drinks manufacturers have a presence within the country so there will be no trouble getting hold of a thirst-quencher. Local brand beers to look out for include Angkor, Angkor Stout and Bayon. Draft Angkor is available in many restaurants as well as beer gardens in Phnom Penh, Sihanoukville and Siem Reap.

Very competitively priced European and Australian wines and spirits are available in the supermarkets of Phnom Penh and Siem Reap. The more upmarket restaurants throughout the country usually have a wine list, not always great, but better than nothing.

Entertainment

Cambodia could never hope to rival its neighbour Thailand for entertainment and nightlife, but it does possess a breadth of cultural activities that ought to satisfy most visitors. Phnom Penh has developed a remarkably unrestrained nightlife while Siem Reap offers a number of more traditional cultural diversions. Sihanoukville's cultural scene is more limited and visitors will have to satisfy themselves with the bars and a string of very good restaurants.

Under the Khmer Rouge there was no room for entertainment whatsoever; today almost anything goes. The downside of Cambodia's market liberalisation and political reforms over the last two decades may well be that things have gone too far the other way with a plethora of seedy bars and massage parlours now open in Phnom Penh and to a lesser extent in Siem Reap and Sihanoukville.

The best sources of information on both traditional Cambodian arts performances and the best bars and nightspots in the country are the English-language Canby Publications (*www.canbypublications.com*) magazines *The Phnom Penh Visitors Guide, The Siem Reap Visitors Guide* and *The Sihanoukville Visitors Guide*. These are distributed free in hotels, guesthouses and restaurants. Another valuable source of listings and general information about the country can be found in the monthly *Bayon Pearnik* magazine

which can also be downloaded at *www.bayonpearnik.com*

The performing arts
Dance

Today, even after the horrors wreaked on this sophisticated art form by Pol Pot and his psychopathic Khmer Rouge regime, the visitor will find the performances well worth seeing. Classical Khmer dance or *lamthon* bears a close resemblance to that of the Thai royal court.

Dancers take years to perfect the many different gestures and dances required for a full performance. Dances usually depict incidents from either the Buddha birth cycle stories, known as the *Jataka*, or from the *Reamker*, Cambodia's very own version of the Indian epic *Ramayana*. Elaborate costumes are the norm with some performers also wearing masks.

A number of hotels in Phnom Penh and Siem Reap offer classical dance performances. Particularly fine troupes in Siem Reap perform at the Raffles Grand Hotel d'Angkor and the Apsara Theatre, part of the Angkor Village Hotel. In Phnom Penh try the excellent Sovanna Phum Theatre.

Shadow puppets

The Cambodians have a tradition of shadow puppetry similar to that found in southern Thailand and the Malay world. This art form is called *nang sbek thom*, or 'shadow plays'. A good time to see puppet performances is during festivals or, if you're lucky enough to be invited, at a wedding. Puppets are made of buffalo or cow hide, and are often very complex. A large screen is erected with light cast onto it from behind. The audience sits in front of the screen and watches the images cast by the puppets.

Music

Today Cambodian traditional music flourishes throughout the country, especially in villages and temples (*see also p17*).

Bars and pubs

Phnom Penh's bar and pub scene is surprisingly lively and spreads across

Cambodian Royal Ballet

Open-air bar and restaurant on Sisowath Quay, Phnom Penh

most of the city. Many places stay open until the early hours. The town offers numerous live music bars and pubs that welcome all-comers as well as the more male-oriented hostess bars. A growing number of lively sports bars, showing all the latest Premier League football and other major sporting events, can be found along Sisowath Quay.

Siem Reap's 'Pub Street' is the heart of the town's nightlife. Bars on this busy street near the Old Market usually have generous happy hours often starting as early as 4pm. Similarly, Sihanoukville's Ekareach Street in the centre of the town hosts some sports bars and other pure drinking dens, a few of which stay open all night. Live music can be heard in one or two places on Weather Station Hill where there are also a few hostess bars.

Cafés

Pavement cafés are a very agreeable hangover from French colonial days. Many are found along the riverfront on Sisowath Quay in Phnom Penh. Usually open from the early morning, they are great places to start the day off with a good cup of coffee and perhaps a warm croissant. A smaller café scene also thrives in Siem Reap mainly around the Old Market area by the Siem Reap River.

Cinema

In the 1950s and 60s Cambodia was home to a surprisingly lively local film scene. King Sihanouk himself was an avid movie fan and in the 1960s began making films which he wrote, directed and sometimes starred in, one of his most famous being *Apsara* (1966). These days, mainly due to lack of money and resources, the scene is nowhere near as vibrant, with low-budget horror films being the staple. There are a few independent film companies struggling to make their way, but they constantly face the challenge of almost total lack of copyright and intellectual property law enforcement plus the easy availability of counterfeit DVDs.

As far as actual cinemas in Cambodia, there are virtually none. The **French Cultural Centre** (*218 Keo Chea Street. Tel: (023) 213 124*) does screen the occasional French film, but most Hollywood productions are counterfeited almost as soon as they come out, copies appearing indecently quickly in many tourist cafés and bars.

Art galleries

A thriving contemporary art scene now exists in Cambodia, especially in Phnom Penh. The representational arts, particularly painting, broadly fit into two traditions. Some artists, usually older, stick with the traditional methods used in Khmer art over many centuries, whereas a number of younger artists have combined traditional Khmer art with Western modernism, creating a breathtaking array of dynamic, inspired canvases. Several galleries in the capital have sprung up over the last few years to promote modern Cambodian art and you can find advertisements for their many and varied showings in Canby Publications' *The Phnom Penh Visitors Guide.*

The Foreign Correspondents Club of Cambodia bar and restaurant

Shopping

Cambodia is not recognised worldwide for its shopping, but it does in fact have some excellent bargains and a wide range of unusual handicrafts and antiques. With its traditional markets, Phnom Penh offers the greatest potential, with Siem Reap a close second. The country produces some particularly fine silver work and much of the silk produced is as good as anywhere in the world.

Prices are generally reasonable in Cambodia. Traditionally, you would be expected to haggle, and this is still the case in markets and street souvenir shops. By contrast haggling is not expected in fixed-price places such as the new, air-conditioned shopping malls in Phnom Penh.

In traditional markets the sound of bargaining is commonplace. Shops selling the same items often cluster together in one street and markets have stall after stall specialising in similar goods. You may get a better price by enquiring at each stall and hoping prices fall as the vendors undercut one another. Remember when haggling to always smile and be polite; you'll get a better price, while at the same time making the traders around you pleased, even if they don't make a sale.

Locals tend to shop for groceries early in the morning, so if you're intending doing a little market shopping it's best to visit in the afternoon when the traders have cooled off. In the cities, shopping hours are usually 7.30–11.30am and 1.30–4.30pm, but increasingly shops and malls stay open until 6.30pm or later.

What to buy
Antiques

In Phnom Penh, the Tuol Tom Pong Market, also known as the Russian Market, offers the widest selection of antiques and pseudo-antiques. In Siem Reap try the Psar Chas or Old Market south of the former French Quarter, and the shops in the surrounding area. Some high-quality wood and stone carvings are available, as are attractively worked metal heads of Jayavarman VII. Beautifully executed rubbings of bas-reliefs are for sale at very reasonable prices in the market. Authentic antiquities from Angkor should not be purchased and/or exported under any circumstances, though needless to add the trade in looted art treasures continues, despite the best efforts of the authorities.

Gems and jewellery

Pailin is Cambodia's major source of gems, but was largely worked out by the Khmer Rouge in the 1990s who exported the stones to Thailand. Gems and jewellery are available at the Central Market and Tuol Tom Pong Market in Phnom Penh.

Silk

Takeo Province to the south of Phnom Penh is the silk weaving centre of the country; however, you will find family weaving ventures all over Cambodia. It's possible to purchase long lengths of silk for making into blouses or dresses on your return home, or have them specially made up at one of the many tailor shops found just about everywhere. An alternative is to purchase one of the beautifully woven silk *kramaa*, or scarves, that have become synonymous with Khmer cultural identity. Almost every market sells *kramaa* in a variety of cloths.

Silver

The country produces some excellent silver belts, jewellery and other silver filigree work. Many of Cambodia's finest silversmiths are Cham Muslims, working in villages north of Phnom Penh. Good places to find silver gifts include the Tuol Tom Pong Market and Central Market in Phnom Penh, and the Old Market in Siem Reap.

Ceramics at Tuol Tom Pong Market, Phnom Penh

Sport and leisure

Outdoor sport can be a hot and sweaty pastime in tropical Cambodia; nevertheless, plenty of Cambodians brave the heat and step outside to do some form of exercise most days. In the early evenings groups of young men and boys can be seen playing football or sepak takraw *(a traditional Southeast Asian game involving a rattan ball) in most parts of the country.*

Participatory sports

Most of Cambodia's top hotels have a fitness centre, a swimming pool and tennis courts. Some have evolved into spas and offer massage and other therapeutic treatments. Non-residents can often use the facilities by paying an entrance fee or by becoming a member of the hotel's club.

Golf in Cambodia is becoming more popular with the small but expanding middle class and like in so many other countries acts as an extension of the boardroom where deals are made between shots. The game has long been popular with the ruling elite and Prime Minister Hun Sen is reputedly quite a good player.

For the visitor there are a few good courses open around Phnom Penh and Siem Reap. Just off National Route 4, 30km (19 miles) from Phnom Penh, the Cambodia Golf and Country Club was the country's first course. In Siem Reap, the Phokeethra Country Club, 16km (10 miles) outside the town, is presently Cambodia's best course.

As in neighbouring Thailand and Malaysia, snooker has become a very popular pastime over the last couple of decades. Snooker parlours have popped up everywhere and costs are extremely low compared to similar facilities in the United Kingdom.

Sepak takraw is popular across Cambodia

In the air-conditioned parlours tables and cues can be of the highest quality. Unfortunately, non-AC places can leave a little to be desired as cues tend to warp and tables buckle in the heat.

On the coast diving has become a passion. Sihanoukville offers plenty of opportunities to get under the sea and visit the offshore coral or the shipwrecks further afield. Canby Publications' English-language magazine *The Sihanoukville Visitors Guide* lists a number of internationally recognised scuba diving operators (*www.canbypublications.com*).

Other water sports in Sihanoukville include parasailing, water-skiing, jet-skiing, kayaking and wind surfing, all available through the more upmarket resorts.

Again, on the coast, deep-sea fishing is an exciting prospect for the adventurous and offers numerous challenges. With the waters of the Gulf of Thailand teeming with barracuda, king mackerel, sailfish, tuna and wahoo, a day's fishing can be a memory to treasure.

Spectator sports

Kickboxing is said to have originated in Cambodia and, as in neighbouring Thailand, is one of the country's most popular spectator sports. Regular bouts are televised every week.

The Phnom Penh National Olympic Stadium plays host to regular football matches and tournaments and although Cambodian football is not of a

Golf is becoming more popular with Cambodia's growing middle class

particularly high standard matches can be fun to watch.

Both a participatory sport and a spectator sport, *sepak takraw*, as it is commonly known across Southeast Asia, is both enjoyable to watch and play. Realistically though, to play you need some years of practice. The game involves a ball resembling a volleyball made of rattan, a net and two teams of three people. The idea is for each team to knock the ball across the net to the other team using only the foot or head without the ball hitting the ground. Each team is only allowed three attempts at getting the ball across the net, otherwise the opposition scores a point. *Takraw* games can often be seen in the evenings at temple festivals.

Children

Cambodia is not the best place to travel with children and should probably not be your first destination for accustoming the family to the pleasures of travel. The lack of specific children's attractions and the unfamiliarity of the food can make this a challenge for all but the hardiest. Having said that, a few days exploring the ruins at Angkor coupled with a week at the beach ought to satisfy older children.

In Phnom Penh there are a few activities that should keep the kids happy for a while. **The Phnom Penh Water Park** (*50 Pochentong Rd. Tel: (023) 881 008. Open: daily 9.30am–6pm. Admission charge*) has slides, pools, water jets and fountains, all great fun, especially if the weather is particularly hot. In Siem Reap there are plans to build a huge 35-hectare (86-acre) water and entertainment park called Kingdom of Dreams. The park will include an IMAX theatre, hotel and large restaurant. To be built in two phases, the water park is expected to be finished sometime in late 2008.

Young and old children should find the delightful puppet shows at the **Sovanna Phum Theatre** (*111, Street 360 (corner of Street 105). Tel: (023) 987 564. Performances: Fri and Sat 7.30pm. Admission charge*) most entertaining.

The 12-lane **Super Bowl** bowling alley (*2nd Floor, Parkway Centre, 191 Mao Tse Tung Boulevard. Tel: (023) 982 928. Open: 10am–10.30pm. Admission charge*) makes a great place to spend the afternoon in air-conditioned luxury. There's also a decent range of food and drink opportunities within the complex.

There are plenty of good swimming pools around the capital that accept visitors; in fact many of the better hotels in town welcome families for a small fee. The **Raffles Hotel Le Royal** (*92 Rukhak Vithei Daun Penh (off Monivong Boulevard), Sangkat Wat Phnom. Tel: (023) 981 888*) has its own children's pool as well as a larger, adult-sized pool. Other welcoming places include the **Billabong Hotel** (*5, Street 158. Tel: (023) 223 703*) and the **Himawari Hotel** (*313 Sisowath Quay. Tel: (023) 214 555*).

In Siem Reap activities related purely to children are even more limited than in Phnom Penh, although most youngsters will enjoy clambering around Angkor's temple ruins and climbing to the pinnacle of Angkor Wat. If they've seen Angelina Jolie in

Tomb Raider then they should have a great time, especially in Ta Prohm's root-encased ruins.

A fun way to watch the sun set at Angkor is take an elephant ride from the base of Phnom Bakheng just outside Angkor Thom's south gate, up the hill. The fare includes the return trip down.

Another Angkor-related activity that most children ought to get pretty excited about is the 10-minute hot-air balloon ride at the front of Angkor Wat. The balloon is tethered a short distance to the west of the entrance to Angkor Wat and rises to around 200m (660ft). The views are wonderful with plenty of photo opportunities.

The Happy Ranch (*2km/1¼ miles*) *east of the Old Market, near Svay Dangkum Pagoda. Tel: (011) 920 002)* outside Siem Reap offers horse riding lessons and trail riding for all ages.

Children will enjoy Ta Prohm, made famous by *Tomb Raider*

Essentials

Arriving and departing
By air

Phnom Penh International Airport is 10km (6 miles) from the centre of the city. The journey into town takes around 30 minutes. Taxis and motorcycle taxis (*moto*) can be hired in front of the arrivals building. The standard fare for a taxi to downtown Phnom Penh is US$7. Motorcycle taxis charge around US$2. Some hotels offer a free pick-up service to and from the airport.

Siem Reap International Airport is 7km (4 miles) from the town. Taxis can be found just outside the terminal building and charge around US$5 for a 15-minute trip to the centre of Siem Reap. Many hotels and guesthouses offer a free taxi service to and from the airport if you have made a reservation in advance.

Domestic airport departure tax is US$6, international US$25.

By road

It is now possible to enter Cambodia by land at a number of crossing points from Laos, Thailand and Vietnam. The trip between Ho Chi Minh City and Phnom Penh, crossing the border at Moc Bai, usually takes about five hours by taxi. The most popular entry point from Thailand remains the Aranya Prathet–Poipet border point.

By sea

Regular speedboats travel between Ban Had Lek in Trat Province, Thailand and Koh Kong Town. From Koh Kong there are several boats leaving for Sihanoukville.

Customs

Cambodian customs regulations are fairly relaxed. Officially each visitor is allowed one bottle of spirits, 200 cigarettes and a reasonable amount of perfume. Visitors are not allowed to import more than US$10,000 in cash, which must be declared on arrival.

Cambodian customs are tough on anybody importing illegal narcotics and pornographic literature.

Electricity

The electricity supply is 220 volts, 50 cycles AC. Several socket types are in use, for which a multiple adaptor plug should be purchased before departure. Power cuts occur frequently throughout the country so it is a good idea to carry a torch.

Internet

Connections are usually fast and costs are low, around US$1 per hour. Internet cafés can be found all over Siem Reap, Phnom Penh and Sihanoukville. Many hotels provide internet access, although it will be more expensive.

Money

The Cambodian unit of currency is the riel. Almost all transactions in tourist areas are made in US dollars, with the exception of very small ones, such as motorcycle taxi rides, which are paid for in riel. Riel notes come in denominations of 100,000, 50,000, 20,000, 10,000, 5,000, 2,000, 1,000, 500, 200 and 100. The import and export of riel is prohibited. The riel is a fairly stable currency and generally trades at around 4,000 to US$1. Thai baht is acceptable in Siem Reap and the Thai border areas.

Credit cards, traveller's cheques and ATMs

Traveller's cheques are difficult to change upcountry with only a few banks in Battambang, Siem Reap and Sihanoukville handling them. They are easier to change in Phnom Penh as many banks will deal with them. US dollar cheques are preferable.

Most hotels and upmarket restaurants will accept Visa and MasterCard when you're paying bills, as will airline offices. Cash advances on cards are possible in certain banks in Phnom Penh, Siem Reap, Battambang and Sihanoukville. Most banks charge a minimum US$5 for any transaction.

Opening hours

Government offices and public institutions open Monday to Saturday from 7.30am until 11.30am and 2pm till 5pm or 6pm. Sunday is usually a holiday. Banks open Monday to Friday, 8.30am to 3.30pm. Some banks and foreign exchange offices may open on Saturday morning. Temples are usually open from around 7am and close their gates between 5pm and 6pm. Markets generally open as early as 6am and function every day of the week. Private businesses, such as shops and restaurants, open from early in the morning until late in the evening, and even into the early hours.

Passports and visas

All visitors to Cambodia must obtain a visa either before or on arrival at Phnom Pehn or Siem Reap airports. One-month visas are issued by Cambodian embassies and consulates around the world. For a visa on arrival one passport picture and US$20 is required; this is then valid for 30 days. If you intend arriving overland then a visa must be obtained either in Bangkok, Ho Chi Minh City or Vientiane.

Pharmacies

Pharmacies are instantly recognisable by their use of the old French medical symbol of a snake wrapped around a long-stemmed glass and are well stocked. They are usually open 7am–8pm. Generally, staff don't have dispensing qualifications. For more serious problems, ask your hotel or guide for assistance with a doctor's visit, or a trip to the local hospital.

Post

Main post offices are open 7am to 7pm, and offer a wide range of postal services. Items take one to two weeks to reach destinations outside Asia, but do so fairly reliably.

Public holidays

1 January	New Year's Day
7 January	Victory over Genocide Day
8 March	International Women's Day
13, 14, 15 April	Cambodian New Year
1 May	Labour Day
May full moon	Visakha Bochea
May	Ploughing of the Holy Furrow Ceremony
18 June	Queen Mother's Birthday
24 September	Constitution Day
Sept/Oct	Bon Pchum Ben
29 October	Coronation Day
31 October	King Father's Birthday
9 November	Independence Day
November	Water Festival
10 December	Human Rights Day

Smoking

Cambodian males are some of the heaviest smokers in the world with up to 86 per cent of men in rural areas smoking. No-smoking areas are rare, but some restaurants do impose restrictions.

Suggested reading and media

The *Phnom Penh Post* is an English-language newspaper printed once a fortnight and is regarded as the newspaper of note. It has an internet presence at *www.phnompenhpost.com*. *The Cambodia Daily*, another English-language title, covers domestic events in some detail. Its international coverage is less comprehensive. International magazines and newspapers including the *Bangkok Post, International Herald Tribune, Newsweek* and *Time* are available from a number of outlets including **Monument Books** (*111 Norodom Boulevard, Phnom Penh. Tel: (023) 217 617. Open: 7.30am–9pm*). *Bayon Pearnik*, a free monthly English-language magazine, contains listings of all local events and the latest restaurants.

Sustainable tourism

Thomas Cook is a strong advocate of ethical and fairly traded tourism and believes that the travel experience should be as good for the places visited as it is for the people who visit them. That's why we firmly support The Travel Foundation, a charity that develops solutions to help improve and protect holiday destinations, their environment, traditions and culture. To find out what you can do to make a positive difference to the places you travel to and the people who live there, please visit *www.thetravelfoundation.org.uk*

Telephones

Calling home from Cambodia

Australia: *001 (or 007) + 61 + area code*

South Africa: *001 (or 007) + 27 +* area code
New Zealand: *001 (or 007) + 64 +* area code
Republic of Ireland: *001 (or 007) + 353* + area code (without first 0)
UK: *001 (or 007) + 44 + area code* (without first 0)
USA and Canada: *001 (or 007) + 1 +* area code

By adding 007 to the beginning of a number the call can be cheaper than using 001.

Calling Cambodia from abroad

To call Cambodia from abroad, dial the access code *00* from the UK, Ireland and New Zealand; *011* from the US and Canada; *0011* from Australia, followed by the country code for Cambodia, *855* and the regional number without the first 0 in the area code.

Mobile phones

Cambodia uses the European GSM mobile telephone system. You can either bring your own phone or buy an inexpensive one in Cambodia for your trip (even second-hand phones are available) then just insert an easily bought prepaid SIM card. You can now receive calls from abroad without paying roaming charges.

Time zone

Cambodia is seven hours ahead of Greenwich Mean Time (GMT). This puts Cambodia seven hours ahead of London, twelve hours ahead of New York and three hours behind Melbourne.

Toilets

Except in tourist areas, public toilets are not usually very good. It is wise to take your own toilet paper or tissues. Toilets in the bigger hotels and restaurants are usually good.

Travellers with disabilities

Lack of facilities, difficulty of access and overloaded transport make life hard for those with mobility problems, although some of the better hotels do make an effort.

For further information, contact:
UK: Royal Association for Disability and Rehabilitation (RADAR), *12 City Forum, 250 City Road, London EC1V 8AF. Tel: (020) 7250 3222.*
US: Society for Accessible Travel & Hospitality, *347 Fifth Avenue, Suite 610, New York, NY 10016. Tel: (1) 212 447 7284.*

CONVERSION TABLE

FROM	TO	MULTIPLY BY
Inches	Centimetres	2.54
Feet	Metres	0.3048
Yards	Metres	0.9144
Miles	Kilometres	1.6090
Acres	Hectares	0.4047
Gallons	Litres	4.5460
Ounces	Grams	28.35
Pounds	Grams	453.6
Pounds	Kilograms	0.4536
Tons	Tonnes	1.0160

To convert back, for example from centimetres to inches, divide by the number in the third column.

Language

The Cambodian language, otherwise known as Khmer, is a Mon-Khmer language (the indigenous language family of Southeast Asia) spoken by most people in Cambodia. It belongs to the Austro-Asiatic group of languages, a group widely spread throughout mainland Southeast Asia. Khmer is a non-tonal language that has borrowed heavily from Chinese, Pali, Sanskrit, Thai and Vietnamese. The script derives from India and has been used since the 7th century AD. Thai script, which to the untrained eye looks similar, was derived from Khmer in the 12th century AD.

Khmer is a difficult language to learn due to the script, although the lack of tones makes it easier for Westerners than, say, Vietnamese or Thai. It is comparatively easy to pick up some basic vocabulary, however, and any such effort will be greatly appreciated by the Cambodians themselves. English is spoken as a second language by many, especially in Phnom Penh, Siem Reap and Sihanoukville.

TRANSPORT

Car	laan
Bus	laan ch'noul
Bus station	kuhnlaing laan ch'noul
Boat	dtook
Train	roht plerng
Airplane	yohn hawh
Bicycle	kohng
Cyclo	see kloa

TIME

Sunday	t'ngai aadteut
Monday	t'ngai jan
Tuesday	t'ngai onggeea
Wednesday	t'ngai bpoot
Thursday	t'ngai bprahoaa
Friday	t'ngai sok
Saturday	t'ngai sao
Today	t'ngai nih
Tomorrow	t'ngai saaik
Yesterday	m'serl menh
Morning	bpreuk
Afternoon	r'sial
Evening	l'ngiat

NUMBERS

One	moo ay
Two	bpee
Three	bey
Four	buon
Five	bpram

Six	bpram moo ay
Seven	bpram bpee
Eight	bpram bey
Nine	bpram buon
Ten	dahp

FOOD AND DRINK

Restaurant	haang bai
Eat	bpisah
Drinking water	dteuk soht
Ice	dteuk kok
Tea	dtae
Coffee	kahfeh
Milk	dteuk daco
Sugar	sko
Rice	bai
Fish	dt'ray
Beef	saich koh
Pork	saich jruk
Chicken	moan
Plate	jahndtiap
Glass	kaehu
Beer	bia

GENERAL PHRASES

Hello	jumreap sooa
How are you?	tau neak sok sapbaiy jea the?
I'm fine	k'nyom sok sapbaiy
Good morning	arun suor sdei
Good afternoon	tiveah suor sdei
Good evening	sayoanh suor sdei
Good night	reahtrey suor sdei
My name is ...	k'nyom tch muoh ...
What is your name?	lok tch muoh ey?
Yes	baat
No	dteh
Please	sohm mehta
Thank you	orgoon
Excuse me	sohm dtoh
Goodbye	leah suhn heuy
I want a ...	k'nyom jang baan ...
How much is ...?	t'lay pohnmaan ...?
Money	loey
Change	dow
Cheap	towk
Expensive	t'lay
What	ey
Who	niak nah
When	bpehl
Where is ...?	noev eah nah ...?
Where	eah nah
Why	haeht ey
What is this?	nih ch'muah ey?
Does anyone speak English?	tii nih mian niak jeh piasah ohngkleh teh?
I don't understand	k'nyom men yooul teh
Bank	tho neea kear
Hospital	mon dtee bpeth
Police station	s'thaanii bpohlis
Toilet	bawngkohn

Emergencies

EMERGENCY TELEPHONE NUMBERS

Accidents/ambulance: *119*
Police: *117*
Fire: *118*
Tourist police: *(012) 942484*
These numbers are valid throughout Cambodia, but outside of Phnom Penh and Siem Reap there may not be anyone who speaks English immediately available.

Medical services

Casualty

Medical treatment for foreigners in Cambodia is not free and can sometimes be expensive. Before receiving treatment at any hospital you should try to contact your insurers to make sure that you are fully covered. Keep your travel insurance documents to hand at all times, as hospitals will need to see these before dispensing any treatment.

Doctors

The bigger cities including Phnom Penh, Battambang, Sihanoukville and Siem Reap will have private hospitals and clinics with English-speaking doctors. Many of these private institutions have been set up by foreign companies. Some pharmacies will have a doctor on their staff.

Health and insurance

It is recommended that travellers keep tetanus and polio vaccinations up to date, and be vaccinated against typhoid and hepatitis A. Precautions against malaria should be taken by all those travelling to rural areas or making river trips. If you are only intending to visit Phnom Penh or Siem Reap it is not necessary to take precautions as these areas are currently malaria-free. Always get up-to-date medical advice several weeks in advance of your trip. Observe food and water hygiene precautions: drink bottled water, and ensure that food is cleanly prepared.

Be sure to take out comprehensive travel insurance before you travel to Cambodia. Travel insurance policies can be purchased through branches of Thomas Cook and most travel agents.

Hospitals

Calmette Hospital
3 Monivong Boulevard, Phnom Penh. Tel: (023) 426 948. Phnom Penh's largest hospital.
International SOS Medical and Dental Clinic
161, Street 51, Phnom Penh. Tel: (023) 216 911. www.internationalsos.com
Royal Angkor International Hospital
National Route 6 (Airport Road), Phum Kasekam, Khum Sra Ngea, Siem Reap. Tel: (063) 761 888. www.royalangkorhospital.com

Safety and crime

Over the last few years Cambodia has become a much safer country for travellers. Phnom Penh itself used to be quite a dangerous city to move around in at night, but stricter policing has made the capital a lot safer. Robberies do still occur, usually involving visitors travelling on the back of a motorcycle taxi or *moto* late at night. The answer is to take a proper taxi back to your hotel if you intend to be late back. In the unlikely event that you should be stopped by a thief, assume he may be armed and hand over whatever valuables you may be carrying.

Pickpocketing and bag slicing occurs, but can be avoided with a few sensible precautions such as carrying only the money you need with you in a front trouser pocket. Prostitution, although illegal, exists in Phnom Penh, Siem Reap and Sihanoukville, and carries the same inherent dangers as anywhere.

In some parts of the country land mines still pose a danger, so always use well-worn paths.

Cambodia has a well-developed and distinctly sleazy sex tourism industry. Health facilities in the Cambodian sex industry scarcely exist, and visitors should stay well clear of bars and brothels catering to sex tourists, most of whom are locals or visitors from elsewhere in East Asia. It's also worth noting that frequenting such establishments can be physically dangerous and expose the visitor to police scams.

Lost property

Airports and the larger bus depots have lost-property offices. You should report any loss of goods to the police.

Police

Cambodia has its own tourist police, but you will only find them in areas regularly frequented by tourists: Phnom Penh, Siem Reap and Sihanoukville. They usually speak good English and are most helpful. Note that you will need a signed and dated report from the police to claim on your travel insurance for any thefts that occur in the country.

Embassies

Embassies in Phnom Penh include:
Australia *Villa 11, R V Senei Vannavaut Oum (Street 254). Tel: (023) 213470.*
Canada *Villa 9, R V Senei Vannavaut Oum (Street 254). Tel: (023) 213470.*
UK *27-29, Street 75. Tel: (023) 427124.*
USA *1, Street 96, Sangkat Wat Phnom. Tel: (023) 728000.*

Cambodian embassies abroad include:
Australia and New Zealand
5 Canterbury Crescent, Deakin, ACT 2600. Tel: (02) 6273 1259.
Canada Consulate of Cambodia *903-168 Chadwick Court, North Vancouver, British Columbia. Tel: (604) 980 1718.*
UK and Ireland *64 Brondesbury Park, Willesden Green, London, NW6 7AT. Tel: (020) 8451 7850.*
USA *4530 16th Street, NW, Washington, DC 20011. Tel: (202) 726 7742.*

Directory

Accommodation price guide

The accommodation prices are based on the cost per person for two people sharing the least expensive double room with en suite bathroom and excluding breakfast.

★   Under US$10
★★   US$10–US$50
★★★   US$50–US$100
★★★★   Above US$100

Eating out price guide

Price ranges are per person for a meal without drinks.

★   Under US$2
★★   US$2–US$10
★★★   US$10–US$50
★★★★   Above US$50

PHNOM PENH

ACCOMMODATION

Capitol Guesthouse ★
An old favourite for backpackers, this is one of Phnom Penh's longest running establishments. Rooms are basic, but clean and comfortable. The Capitol has extended over the years into the surrounding buildings and now includes Capitol 2, Capitol 3 and the Hello Guesthouse.
14AE0, Street 182, Sangkat Beng Prolitt. Tel: (023) 217 627. Fax: (023) 214 104. Email: capitol@online.com.kh

Billabong Hotel ★★
A tastefully decorated, modern hotel, the Billabong sports its own salt water swimming pool. Room rate includes breakfast and airport pick-up.
5, Street 158. Tel/fax: (023) 223 703. Email: info@thebillabonghotel.com. www.thebillabonghotel.com

Boddhi Tree Aram Boutique Hotel ★★
Situated 20m (65ft) from the Royal Palace, the Boddhi Tree Aram is a delight. With just eight large rooms, each with its own en suite bathroom, satellite TV and air-conditioning, this quiet, serene hotel feels more like an upmarket guesthouse.
70, Street 244, Chhay Chomneas. Tel: (0) 16 865 445. Email: boddhitree_pp@hotmail.com. www.boddhitree.com

Scandinavia Hotel ★★
Situated close to Phnom Penh's Independence Monument, this beautifully renovated boutique hotel offers a serene retreat from the city's busy streets. Super chic décor sets off each of the 16 immaculate air-conditioned bedrooms. Facilities include a friendly bar and a salt water pool. With its own gallery space the Scandinavia also hosts regular art exhibitions, highlighting

many of Cambodia's best artists.

4, Street 282. Tel: (023) 214 498. Email: scandinaviahotel@ yahoo.com. www.hotel-scandinavia-cambodia.com

Walkabout Hotel ★★

Situated close to Phnom Penh's bar area, the Walkabout can get a little noisy, but nevertheless it remains a very popular mid-range choice. All rooms have cable TV, fridge and hot shower. The top-of-the-range room, the Deluxe Private Balcony Room, includes a Jacuzzi®. The hotel's restaurant is open 24 hours a day.

On the corner of Streets 51 (The Strip) and 174. Tel: (023) 211 715. Email: walkabout@online.com.kh. www.walkabouthotel.com

Goldiana Hotel ★★★

A large, first-rate, mid-range hotel with 148 rooms. Amenities include a fitness centre, swimming pool, business centre and a very helpful travel information desk. All rooms include satellite television and refrigerator. The larger

rooms include breakfast. Ask at reception about a free transfer to the airport.

10–12, Street 282, Sangkat Boeung Keng Kang 1. Tel/fax: (023) 219 558. Email: reservation-pnh@goldiana.com. www.goldiana.com

Juliana Hotel ★★★

Regarded as Phnom Penh's premier business hotel, the Juliana is a pleasantly efficient mid-range hotel, slightly away from the city centre. Facilities include a health club, sauna and outdoor swimming pool. All rooms have internet access.

16 Juliana, Street 152, Sangkat Veal Vong. Tel/fax: (023) 880 530. Email: reservation@ julianacambodia.com. www.julianacambodia. com

Tai Ming Plaza Hotel ★★★

The Tai Ming Plaza is a solidly comfortable, mid-range hotel with large, airy rooms. All guest rooms are air-conditioned and contain internet connections, mini-bar, satellite television and

refrigerator. If you enjoy a bit of a flutter the hotel's Player's Club, with its roulette tables, slot machines and other gambling opportunities, is open 24 hours a day. The Tai Ming's exceptional Le Jade restaurant serves a selection of Shanghainese dim sum and other excellent Chinese dishes.

281, Norodom Boulevard. Tel: (023) 219 568. Fax: (023) 217 008. www.tm-plaza.com

Hotel Cambodiana ★★★★

A long-established and impressive hotel, the Cambodiana overlooks the confluence of the Sap, Bassac and Mekong Rivers. Facilities include a magnificently situated swimming pool, the Frangipani Spa, a fitness centre, Phnom Penh's premier wine shop and a most tempting bakery. All rooms are spacious and boast cable TV and in-house movies. With a choice of good restaurants this is one of the city's top spots.

313 Sisowath Quay.

Tel: (023) 426 288. Fax: (023) 426 392. Email: luxury@cambodiana.com. kh. www. hotelcambodiana.com

Inter-Continental ★★★★

Wonderful facilities include a first-class spa, fitness centre, sauna and a beautifully designed pool. A five-star hotel with everything you would expect from this worldwide chain. It is, however, located away from the city's major sights.

296 Mao Tse Tung Boulevard. Tel: (023) 424 888. Fax: (023) 424 885. Email: phnompenh@ interconti.com. www.ichotelsgroup.com

Raffles Hotel Le Royal ★★★★

Unquestionably Phnom Penh's finest hotel, and one with a history, having seen a string of foreign visitors including all the big name journalists of the Vietnam War. A regular fixture on the top hotel lists of various travel and leisure magazines, this 1920s hotel is a blend of Art Deco, French and Khmer architectural styles. With its old world charm and location in the heart of the old French Quarter it's difficult to beat.

92 Rukhak Vithei Daun Penh (off Monivong Boulevard), Sangkat Wat Phnom. Tel: (023) 981 888. Fax: (023) 981 168. Email: phnompenh@ raffles.com. www. phnompenh.raffles.com

EATING OUT

Baan Thai Yai ★

Excellent Thai and Khmer food served in a beautiful old Khmer house. They dish up many of the most popular Thai choices including *tom yam kung* (spicy prawn soup) at low tables where traditionally customers sit on the floor.

13, Street 99, Sangkat Boeng Keng Kang. Tel: (023) 362 991. Open: 7am–9.30pm.

California 2 ★

With a great location overlooking the Sap River, the California 2 offers a range of international dishes including Mexican fish tacos, *huevos rancheros* (ranch eggs), burgers, a number of Khmer dishes and one of Phnom Penh's better breakfast menus. If you are staying in their guesthouse breakfast is included in your room rate. The owners are also a very good source for travel and general information concerning all things Cambodian.

317 Sisowath Quay. Tel: (023) 982 182. Open: 7am–10pm.

Billabong ★★

Set next to the Billabong Hotel's salt water swimming pool and shaded by palm trees, this restaurant is renowned for its Thai cuisine, but try their hummus and satay, which are both very good. The attached bar offers a wide choice of cocktails.

5, Street 158. Tel/Fax: (023) 223 703. www. thebillabonghotel.com. Open: 8am–11pm.

Café Rendez-Vous ★★

A popular, long-running establishment next to the river, this Parisian-style pavement café serves some excellent soups, steaks, salads and pizzas. Look out for the blackboard with the day's specials. It's open very early for coffee and croissants.

127 Eo, corner of Sisowath Quay and Street 108. Tel: (023) 986 466. Open: 5.30am–11pm.

Foreign Correspondents Club of Cambodia ★★

A long-running favourite with expatriates, tourists and locals alike, the FCC overlooks the busy confluence of the Sap and Mekong Rivers and as the sun sets it's a great place to watch the fishermen. The food is an excellent mix of Asian and European-influenced flavours; old standards such as beer-battered fish and chips sit next to newer fusion cuisine like Salt and Kampot Pepper Calamari. If you're not hungry it's a great place to just sit and enjoy one of their many ice cold draught or bottled beers.

363 Sisowath Quay. Tel: (023) 724 014. www.fcccambodia.com. Open: 7am–midnight.

Romdeng Restaurant ★★

A not-for-profit training restaurant run by former street children, the Romdeng offers an array of dishes from Cambodia's provinces. Of the more unusual items on the menu the crispy fried spiders from Skuon might pose the biggest challenge, but if you do have the guts to order them you'll not be disappointed. If you can't bring yourself to try this gustatory revelation then perhaps the pork loin stuffed with fresh coconut might be more suitable.

21, Street 278. Tel: (092) 219 565. Open: 11am– 2.30pm & 5.30–10.30pm. Closed Sun.

Restaurant Le Royal ★★★

The Raffles has a number of first-class restaurants, but Le Royal is the best of the lot and is probably Phnom Penh's finest dining experience. Under a fantastically decorated ceiling based on that found in the Dance Pavilion in the Royal Palace, enjoy a selection of elegantly presented Royal Cambodian dishes.

Raffles Hotel Le Royal, 92 Rukhak Vithei Daun Penh (off Monivong Boulevard), Sangkat Wat Phnom. Tel: (023) 981 888. Fax: (023) 981 168. Email: phnompenh@ raffles.com. www. phnompenh.raffles.com. Open: 11.30am–2.30pm & 5–10.30pm.

ENTERTAINMENT

Elephant Bar

A Phnom Penh tradition, the Elephant Bar has played host to a number of celebrities including Jackie Kennedy. On her visit in 1967, the bar created the legendary Femme Fatale cocktail, a mix of champagne and cognac. It's worth splashing out for at least one drink.

Raffles Hotel Le Royal, 92 Rukhak Vithei Daun Penh (off Monivong Boulevard), Sangkat Wat Phnom. Tel: (023) 981 888. www.phnompenh. raffles.com. Open: 10am–11pm.

Sharky's Bar and Restaurant

Now a Phnom Penh institution, Sharky's has over the years transformed itself from a rather seedy pick-up joint to a regular live music

venue. There are still plenty of working girls hanging about, but the atmosphere is friendly and easy-going. Happy hour is from 4pm to 8pm and most nights there are offers on different beers and spirits at different points in the evening.
126, Street 130. Tel: (023) 211 825. www.sharkysofcambodia.com. Open: 6pm–3am.

Sovanna Phum Theatre
This theatre, where Cambodia's traditional arts are being preserved, offers beautiful classical dance performances along with shadow puppetry and folk dancing. It all makes for an entertaining night out.
111, Street 360 (corner Street 105). Tel: (023) 987 564. Performances: Fri & Sat 7.30pm.

Walkabout Bar and Restaurant
The Walkabout never closes. Giant TV screens broadcast major sporting events from around the world and there are a number of pool tables. A good choice of imported beers from Australia,

Laos and Thailand and the restaurant is famous for its excellent 24-hour breakfast. Each week the bar runs what they call the Joker Draw. Buy a US$1 ticket and enter the prize draw. The winning ticket is drawn on a Friday night and jackpots have been as high as US$8,000.
On the corner of Streets 51 (The Strip) and 174. Tel: (023) 211 715. Email: walkabout@online.com.kh. www.walkabouthotel.com. Open: 24 hours.

SPORT AND LEISURE
Cambodia Golf and Country Club
Cambodia's first 18-hole golf course was opened in 1996 and remains one of the country's few courses. Non-members are welcome although a round will set you back a minimum of US$80. Facilities are excellent and the clubhouse restaurant serves a good mix of Asian and Western dishes.
Off National Route 4, 30km (19km) south of Phnom Penh.

Tel: (023) 363 666. Fax: (023) 212 036.

Champei Spa and Salon
Just like in neighbouring Thailand, the spa boom has hit Phnom Penh. The Champei Spa is one of the best in town and offers relaxing Khmer herbal massages, coconut body scrubs and papaya body polishes along with a host of other healthy treatments.
38, Street 57. Tel: (023) 222 846. Fax: (023) 223 861. Email: info@champeispa.com. www.champeispa.com. Open: 9am–7pm.

NORTH OF PHNOM PENH

Kompong Cham

ACCOMMODATION

Mekong Hotel ★
Kompong Cham's best hotel overlooks the Mekong River, of which the riverside rooms afford some excellent views. All rooms are spacious with a mix of fans and air-conditioning plus very good hot water bathrooms. The downstairs restaurant provides fairly good breakfasts, but you may

find the rest a bit disappointing.
56 Sihanouk Road.
Tel: (042) 941 536.
Fax: (023) 991 866.

EATING OUT
Hao An Restaurant ★★
Food in Kompong Cham is very average, but the Hao An does rise slightly above the ordinary. A mix of Khmer and standard Chinese dishes can be chosen from a picture menu. There's also plenty of cold beer to accompany your meal; the busy beer girls are very attentive.
Preah Monivong Boulevard. Tel: (012) 941 234. Open: 8am–11pm.

SOUTH OF PHNOM PENH
Takeo
ACCOMMODATION
Boeng Takeo Guesthouse ★
Probably the most tourist-friendly place in town and in a very good location next to the lake, the Boeng Takeo offers reasonably comfortable rooms with air-conditioning and satellite television. The

guesthouse prepares breakfast, lunch and dinner on request.
Next to Takeo Lake, on the corner of Streets 3 and 14 .
Tel: (032) 931 306.

EATING OUT
Restaurant Stung Takeo ★★
Serving mainly Khmer dishes, this friendly, stilted restaurant is the best option in Takeo. In the rainy season a large lake forms in front of the establishment and fish become plentiful. It's no revelation that at this time of the year the fish dishes are particularly good.
At the junction of Street 4 and 9. Tel: (016) 957 897. Open: 10am–11pm.

THE COAST
Kampot
ACCOMMODATION
Bokor Mountain Lodge ★★
This beautifully restored old French colonial building has spacious rooms with a choice of air-conditioning or fan. Most rooms overlook the river and are equipped

with cable TV. Other facilities include a good restaurant. Breakfast is included in the room rate.
Riverside Road, south end of town beyond the bridge.
Tel: (033) 932 314.
Email: bokorlodge@gmail. com. www.bokorlodge.com

Rikitikitavi ★★
Well located in a quiet corner of the town next to the river, this relatively recent addition to Kampot's accommodation scene is actually a converted rice barn. All rooms are equipped with bathroom, cable TV and either fan or air-conditioning depending on your preference.
Riverside Road, south end of town. Tel: (012) 235 102. Email: rikitikitavi@asia.com. www.rikitikitavi-kampot.com

EATING OUT
Rikitikitavi ★★
With great views of the Elephant Mountains away across the Tek Chou River to the west, Rikitikitavi cooks up some surprisingly good food. Special dishes include

Cracked Pepper Chicken, Steak and Guinness® Pie, Spicy Beef Spring Rolls and wonderful garlic mushrooms, quite an eclectic mix for a town not really recognised for its gastronomic delicacies. *Riverside Road, south end of town.*
Tel: (012) 235 102.
Open: 7am–11pm.

Kep

ACCOMMODATION

Botanica ★

The Botanica is basic but welcoming, with five comfortable bungalows and a very unusual restaurant. Facilities include a small bar, bicycle rental service, a pool table and what the management dubs a 'world kitchen', serving dishes from as far afield as Algeria, Belgium, Peru and Indonesia. *National Route 33, 2km (1¼ miles) north of the Crab Market.*
Tel: (016) 562 775. Email: info@kep-botanica.com. www.kep-botanica.com

Kep Lodge ★★

An intimate, family-friendly place with just six thatched bungalows, the Lodge offers a holiday surrounded by nature. All bungalows have spacious patios and afford wonderful views of the nearby islands. The restaurant serves some Swiss specialities and the bar area has a pool table. Rates include breakfast.
Pepper Street. Tel: (092) 435 330. Email: info@keplodge.com. www.keplodge.com

Veranda Natural Resort ★★

Superbly located on a hillside overlooking the Gulf of Thailand, the Veranda Natural Resort offers a choice of 15 luxury bungalows, some of which are air-conditioned; others come with just a fan, but all at very reasonable rates. Each bungalow has its own private terrace. With the additions of the Jungle Restaurant and Jungle Bar, the Veranda is a great bargain.
Kep Mountain Hillside Road. Tel: (012) 888 619. Email: verandaresort@ mobitel.com.kh. www.veranda-resort.com

Sihanoukville (Kompong Som)

ACCOMMODATION

Beach Club Resort ★★

Situated close to Sihanoukville's popular Ochheuteal Beach, the Beach Club offers good mid-range accommodation and a decent restaurant. Other facilities include a pool, cocktail bar and helpful tour desk. All rooms contain cable TV and wifi internet.
23 Tola Street, Ochheuteal Beach. Tel: (034) 933 634. Email: beachclub@ camintel.com

Cloud 9 ★★

Fairly basic wooden bungalows in an attractive tropical garden overlooking a quiet part of Serendipity Beach, Cloud 9 makes a pleasant change from the concrete and steel of most resorts in the area. All bungalows have fans, mosquito nets and private bathrooms, and afford great views of the ocean.
Serendipity Beach, next to Sokha Beach. Tel: (012) 479 365. Email: joe.imke @cloud9bungalows.com.

www.cloud9bungalows.
com

Deva Raja Villa ★★

A stylish, intimate hotel, the Deva Raja is new to the Sihanoukville accommodation scene. It's conveniently situated just three minutes from the beach and in the opposite direction lie the bars and restaurants of the Golden Lions roundabout. The bedrooms are spacious and each is tastefully decorated with original works from a variety of Southeast Asian artists. Other amenities include air-conditioning, cable TV and en suite bathroom. There are also a few bungalows for rent. *Ochheuteal Beach Road, between Serendipity and Ochheuteal beaches. Tel: (012) 160 374. Email: myroom@ devarajavilla.com. www.devarajavilla.com*

Holiday Palace Hotel ★★

A large, soulless place with one unique feature: it's a casino, so if you wish to try your luck at a bit of baccarat, blackjack or poker this is the place for you. There are also slot machines dotted around the premises. All rooms are air-conditioned with satellite TV and mini-bars. The restaurant serves a few Khmer favourites and some basic Western dishes. *Krong Street, Victory Beach. Tel: (034) 933 808. Fax: (034) 933 809. Email: holiday_palace02 @yahoo.com*

Reef Resort ★★★

Advertises itself as 'Sihanoukville's premier boutique hotel' and this is a soubriquet it can wear with pride. Excellent value for the facilities available, which include a salt water swimming pool, poolside bar, wireless internet, DVD players in family rooms and a superb restaurant that serves a smattering of Mexican dishes. *Ochheuteal Beach Road, 150m (165yds) from the Golden Lions Monument. Tel: (012) 315 338. Email: bookings@ reefresort.com.kh. www.reefresort.com.kh.*

Independence Hotel ★★★★

One of Sihanoukville's oldest establishments and recently renovated, the Independence sits proudly on its own private beach. From a distance this tall structure looks incongruous and ugly, but it does have some fine amenities including an attractive pool, fitness centre and a number of good restaurants and bars. *Street 2 Thnou, Sangkat 3, Independence Beach. Tel: (034) 934 300. Fax: (034) 933 660. Email: info@ independencehotel.net. www.independencehotel. net*

Sokha Beach Resort ★★★★

A huge, sprawling property on Sokha Beach and the finest accommodation in Sihanoukville, the Sokha provides outstanding facilities including a gym, tennis courts, fitness centre and an excellent spa. It's also one of the few hotels in Cambodia that pays attention to children with its Children's Playground and Sokha Kids-Club. All bedrooms are capacious and tastefully decorated.

Street 2 Thnou, Sokha Beach. Tel: (034) 935 999. Fax: (034) 935 888. Email: reservations@ sokhahotels.com. www.sokhahotels.com

EATING OUT

Starfish Bakery and Café ★

This unpretentious little café in a traditional old Khmer wooden house serves some of the best coffee, cakes and cookies in town. Filling breakfasts with great homemade bread, salads, pastries and scones are also available. The friendly Khmer women that run the café will make up packed lunches on request.

Off Makara Street, behind Samudera Market, town centre. Tel: (012) 952 011. Open: 8am–6pm.

Happy Herb Pizza ★★

The third branch of the successful Phnom Penh chain, the other ones are in Siem Reap and Sihanoukville. It's not just pizzas, although they are very good; you'll also find some interesting Khmer dishes such as beef *lok*

lak, fish *amok* and Khmer Fried Rice. The selection of sandwiches includes BLTs, Italian-subs and Super-subs, each with your choice of baguette, wholewheat or white bread.

81 Ekareach Street. Tel: (012) 632 198. Open: 10am–11pm.

Reef Resort ★★

An excellent selection of Western dishes including steaks, schnitzels and a variety of pasta dishes all set off by a good range of red and white wines. The recent addition of a Mexican menu, quesadillas, tacos and fajitas, makes the Reef a great dining option. If it's just a drink you want the bar stocks more than 80 different beers, wines and spirits.

Ochheuteal Beach Road, 150m (490 ft) from the Golden Lions Monument. Tel: (012) 315 338. Open: 7am–11pm.

Snake House ★★

Here's a place that's not for the squeamish – how about a meal surrounded by some of the world's deadliest snakes? Even the dining tables have

snakes beneath the glass tops; it's all a bit unnerving. Watch out for the crocodile on a leash in the middle of the restaurant. The Russian-owned Snake House serves a mixture of Russian favourites and international standards and it's a lot of fun.

Between North and South Victory Beaches, close to Independence Square. Tel: (012) 673 805. Open: 11am–11pm.

Treasure Island ★★

This large beachside seafood restaurant overlooks Pos Island, and is a lovely place to have dinner and watch the sun set. Dining takes place in a number of open-air pavilions and regulars believe this is the best place in Sihanoukville for fresh seafood, which is no surprise as there are aquariums all over the restaurant teeming with the fruits of the ocean.

Koh Pos Beach, between the Independence Hotel and Hawaii Beach. Tel: (012) 755 335. Open: 10am–10pm.

Le Vivier de la Paillote ★★

A quiet, romantic setting high up on Weather Station Hill, this mainly French restaurant is one of Sihanoukville's better establishments. It's not a big menu, but there's a choice of modern and traditional French favourites, and the various grills are particularly good. There are also a number of seafood dishes. A fine selection of wines complements the food.
Weather Station Hill, Victory Beach.
Tel: (012) 632 347.
Open: 6am–11pm.

SPORT AND LEISURE

Diving and More

With a team of diving instructors hailing from all over the world, Diving and More provide a very professional introduction to the Sihanoukville coastal waters. All levels of expertise are welcome, from total novice to experienced PADI-qualified regular diver.
Sopheak Meangul Road, corner of Street 108.
Tel/Fax: (034) 934 220.

Email: info@ divingandmore.com.
www.divingandmore.com

Scuba Nation Diving Centre

The Scuba Nation offers specially tailored diving trips that even include midnight dives along with daily diving courses. All instructors are fully trained and come from Europe, Australia and North America.
Mohachai Guesthouse, Serendipity Beach Road.
Tel: (034) 933 700.
Email:
scubanation@yahoo.com.
www.divecambodia.com

Seeing Hands Massage

Traditional massage performed by trained, sight-impaired masseuses. A one-hour session will cost in the region of US$3 and if you've got any aches and pains they will find them.
95 Ekareach Street.
Tel: (012) 799 016.
Open: 8am–9pm.

Tradewinds Charters

Exciting deep-sea fishing trips organised through one of Sihanoukville's most popular bars. They provide all the necessary fishing gear and a

comfortable 16½m (54ft) Western-style boat. The seas around Sihanoukville are full of fascinating marine life and there's a chance you might catch a marlin or even a shark.
Fisherman's Den Sports Bar, off Sopheakmonkol Street, opposite the Caltex Station. Tel: (034) 933 997. Email:
nzbrian@camintel.com

ANGKOR

Siem Reap

ACCOMMODATION

Chez Om ★★

With a series of small villas and detached houses positioned around a striking tropical garden, the Chez Om offers traditional Cambodian hospitality in the perfect setting. The establishment's Baray Petit Garden Restaurant prides itself on providing traditional Khmer dishes made only with natural ingredients. This place definitely makes a change from the larger new concrete hotels that seem to be going up every month in Siem Reap.
South end of town, 200m (220yd) from the

Build Bright University. Tel: (012) 587 045. Email: info@chezom.com. www.chezom.com

Earthwalkers ★★

Set up by a group of young Norwegians, Earthwalkers strives to give something back to the neighbourhood by re-investing part of the profits in local community projects. With just 20 rooms, a mix of fan and AC, and in a secluded countryside environment, the onus is on relaxation and calm. Free airport, ferry or bus terminal pick-up.

Sala Kanseng Village, just off National Route 6. Tel: (012) 967 901. Email: mail@earthwalkers.no. www.earthwalkers.no

L'Eurasiane ★★

Located in a quiet area to the east of the Old Market, this atmospheric old wooden Khmer house offers just four exquisitely decorated rooms and one luxurious suite. Each room is named after a tropical flower and is equipped with air-conditioning, satellite TV and its own private terrace. The

owners will organise all your taxi needs including pick-up from either the airport or the port.

100m (110yd) beyond Wat Bo Street, southeast corner of town. Tel: (012) 677 622. E-mail: eurasiane@online.com.kh. www.eurasiane-angkor. com

Secrets of Elephants Inn ★★

This low-key establishment with a great name is full of beautiful old wooden furniture and Buddha figures. Rooms are not the most comfortable but the intimacy of the whole place makes up for this; it's more like staying in a private home. Rates include breakfast.

National Route 6. Tel: (063) 964 328. Email: info@angkor-travel.com. www.angkor-travel.com

Shadow of Angkor ★★

Housed in an old French colonial building in the Psar Chaa area overlooking the Siem Reap River, the Shadow of Angkor offers great value and has been a popular choice for many years. Rooms vary in size and

come with a mix of fan and air-conditioning, but all contain satellite TV. The restaurant serves an excellent mix of Khmer and international dishes. Internet is available.

353 Pokambor Avenue. Tel/Fax: (063) 964 774. Email: shadowofangkor@ hotmail.com. www. shadowofangkor.com

Angkor Village Hotel ★★★

This quiet and secluded hotel on the east side of the Siem Reap River consists of traditional Khmer-style dwellings surrounded by lotus-filled pools and finely manicured gardens. Facilities include an attractive outdoor pool, business centre and a particularly helpful tour desk. The hotel also offers guests the chance to become elephant handlers for a few days at the Angkor Mahout Academy.

Wat Bo Road. Tel: (063) 965 561. Fax: (063) 965 565. Email: welcome@ angkorvillage.com. www.angkorvillage.com

Bopha Angkor ★★★

The Bopha is excellent value considering the

number of first-class facilities on site. It's set in beautiful lush tropical gardens with attractive bungalows dotted around. The main building is a beautifully restored French colonial structure. Facilities include a striking swimming pool and a popular restaurant serving Cambodian and international cuisine.

512 Acharsvar Road.
Tel: (063) 964 928.
Fax: (063) 964 446.
Email: bopharesa@bopha-angkor.com.
www.bopha-angkor.com

Princess Angkor Hotel ★★★

One of a number of good hotels situated conveniently on the Airport Road. The Princess offers excellent value considering the wide range of facilities on site, including massage centre, spa, swimming pool and lovely lawns. If you arrive in the evening you can't miss the place; it's lit up like a Christmas tree.

National Route 6, Airport Road. Tel: (063) 760 056.

Fax: (063) 963 668.
Email: info@princessangkor.com.
www.princessangkor.com

Shinta Mani ★★★

This splendidly restored colonial mansion in the centre of the former French Quarter offers superb facilities including cooking classes. It also holds art exhibitions and provides vocational training to those less fortunate in the local community. The beautifully designed rooms are an airy delight.

Junction of Oum Khum and 14th Street.
Tel: (063) 761 998.
Fax: (063) 761 999.
Email: reservations@shintamani.com.
www.shintamani.com

Angkor Palace Resort and Spa ★★★★

A five-star, Cambodian-owned, luxury hotel with a range of stylish rooms. The Angkor Palace offers all the conveniences of a top-flight hotel including a large spa, steam room and sauna, fitness centre, outdoor Jacuzzi® and tennis courts. The excellent Soriya restaurant

serves a delightful mix of Cambodian and international dishes in a traditional Khmer setting. Nightly cultural shows are held in a specially designed pavilion.

555 Khum Svay Dang Khum. Tel: (063) 760 511.
Fax: (063) 760 512.
Email: info@angkorpalaceresort.com.
www.angkorpalaceresort.com

Apsara Angkor Hotel ★★★★

Superbly outfitted rooms with every modern convenience imaginable including climate controlled air-conditioning (lovely after a hot day scrambling around the ruins), cable television and your own fancy bathrobe. Special mention should be made of the disabled facilities, not a common feature in this part of the world. It's well situated for the airport.

National Route 6, Airport Road.
Tel: (063) 964 999.
Fax: (063) 964 567.
Email: hotel@apsaraangkor.com.
www.apsaraangkor.com

Angkor Howard Hotel ★★★★

One of Siem Reap's recent luxury additions, the sumptuous Angkor Howard provides excellent lodgings. With 308 rooms there's no chance of them being overbooked. Amenities include a beautiful swimming pool surrounded by a lush tropical garden. The fitness centre contains the very latest in exercise equipment and the spa provides a welcome break after an exhausting day clambering around the old temples.

National Route 6, Airport Road. Tel: (063) 965 000. Fax: (063) 965 111. E-mail: info@ angkorhoward.com. www.angkorhoward.com

Raffles Grand Hotel d'Angkor ★★★★

This, the oldest and most graceful hotel in Siem Reap, is the Raffles Group's flagship hotel in Cambodia. The building is a French colonial work of art and sits in the centre of Siem Reap opposite King Sihanouk's villa. Since its complete restoration a few years ago it consistently wins awards from all over the world and can rightly claim to be one of Southeast Asia's grandest hotels. Even if you're not staying here it's certainly worth a visit to sample the delights of either the Elephant Bar or the Café d'Angkor.

1 Vithei Charles de Gaulle, Khum Svay Dang Kum. Tel: (063) 963 888. Fax: (063) 963 168. Email: siemreap@raffles.com. www.siemreap.raffles.com

EATING OUT

Dead Fish Tower ★★

A genuine Siem Reap oddity, the Dead Fish Tower has its own crocodile pool and a fine choice of Khmer, Thai and international dishes. In the evening traditional Khmer dancers entertain customers along with a number of live bands.

Sivatha Boulevard. Tel: (012) 630 377. Open: 7am–1am.

Kampuccino Pizza ★★

Just around the corner from the Old Bazaar, in a delightful setting next to the Siem Reap River, the Kampuccino has been around for a number of years and for good reason, as it serves some of the best pizzas in town. But it's not just the pizzas; the extensive menu manages to cover just about every area of the gastronomic globe.

362 Pokambor Avenue. Tel: (012) 970 896. Open: 7am–midnight.

The Red Piano ★★

One of Siem Reap's most enduring and popular restaurants, the Red Piano offers a variety of steaks and pastas as well as a fine wine list and a number of cocktails. The upstairs balcony is a great place to sit and watch the action down on Pub Street. Try one of their 'Tomb Raider' cocktails, supposedly first consumed by Hollywood actress Angelina Jolie on location a few years ago. It also serves good breakfasts.

50m (55yd) northwest of the Old Bazaar (Psar Chas) on the corner of Pub Street.

Tel: (063) 963 240.
Open: 7am–midnight.

FCC Angkor Kitchen ★★★

The younger sister of the more famous Foreign Correspondents Club in Phnom Penh, the FCC in Siem Reap is situated close to the river amid some beautiful old rain trees. Here you'll find some of the finest food available in Siem Reap including wonderfully crisp spring rolls, beef *lok lak*, grilled Australian sirloin, and kaffir lime and coconut brûlée.

Pokambor Avenue.
Tel: (063) 760 280.
www.fcccambodia.com.
Open: 7am–midnight.

Sawasdee ★★★

If you're looking for something a bit spicier than traditional Khmer cuisine, this delightful Thai restaurant is the answer. Choose from indoor air-conditioned comfort or the pleasant garden seating. The enormous menu includes a profusion of fiery Thai-style salads, curries and aromatic soups, as well as plenty of vegetarian options. They do Western breakfasts as well, but they are no match for the Thai food.

25 Wat Bo Road.
Tel: (063) 964 456.
Open: 6.30am–10pm.

Viroth's ★★★

A stylish, contemporary setting for some distinctively modern Cambodian cooking, Chef Viroth has created some masterpieces including an excellent chicken *amok* and is usually around to elucidate on the subtleties of his fine Khmer cuisine. Desserts include a variety of cakes and ice cream.

246 Wat Bo Road. Tel: (016) 951 800. Open: 11am–2.30pm & 5.30pm–11pm.

Entertainment

Apsara Theatre

A number of hotels offer classical Cambodian dance performances in Siem Reap and it's hard to choose one over another. The Angkor Village Hotel offers a splendid meal to accompany the dancing. Performances include a number of different dances embracing ordinary folk culture, from the Fishermen's Dance, to the high Royal culture of the *Reamker* (the Khmer version of the Indian classic *Ramayana*). Costumes are exquisite.

Angkor Village Hotel, Wat Bo Road. Tel: (063) 965 561. Email: welcome@ angkorvillage.com. www.angkorvillage.com. Performances: daily 6.30pm and 8pm.

Temple Club

With its very good sound system, as well as a sports TV room, the Temple plays host to a constant flow of night-time revellers. The small dance floor heats up after midnight to the sounds of a live DJ. On a more traditional note, there's also nightly Apsara dance performances upstairs between 7.30pm and 9.30pm. Happy Hour usually stretches from around 4pm to as late as 9pm.

Pub Street, northwest of the Old Bazaar (Psar Chas).
Tel: (015) 999 909.
Open: 7am–3am.

Sport and leisure

Bodia Spa

A haven dedicated to sensory experience, the Bodia offers head, back and shoulder massages, hot stone massage and reflexology. The on-site juice bar is a plus and they organise regular yoga classes.

Above U-Care Pharmacy, close to (Pub Street), northwest of the Old Bazaar (Psar Chaa). Tel: (063) 761 593. www.bodia-spa.com. Open: 9am–7pm.

Phokeethra Country Club

Located just 16km (10 miles) from downtown Siem Reap, this first-class 18-hole course is the best in the country. Visitors are welcome.

Vithei Charles de Gaulle, Khum Svay Dang Kum. Tel: (063) 964 600. www.phokeethragolf.com

Battambang

Accommodation

Bus Stop Guesthouse ★★

A clean, comfortable new option in Battambang, all rooms are air-conditioned with satellite TV and en suite bathroom. They also claim the fastest internet connection in town. The Bus Stop doubles as a popular bar with live sport and the basic restaurant serves decent breakfasts.

149, Street 3, next door to the White Rose Restaurant. Tel: (053) 730 544. Email: info@ busstopcambodia.com. www.busstopcambodia. com

La Villa ★★★

This superbly restored 1930s French colonial villa was used by the Vietnamese army after the overthrow of the Khmer Rouge in 1979. It's now a cosy six-bedroom gem. Art Deco furnishings and antiques leave the impression of a bygone age. All bedrooms contain canopied four-poster beds, satellite TV and air-conditioning.

185 Pom Romchek 5 Kom. Tel: (053) 730 151. Email: lavilla@online.com.kh. www.lavilla-battambang.com

Eating out

White Rose ★

A mind-bogglingly extensive menu reveals authentic Khmer favourites (rice porridge with pork), Chinese standards (sweet and sour chicken), Thai spicy specials and a number of popular Western dishes. The owners are friendly and will provide takeaway Cambodian-style baguettes. The fruit shakes served here are particularly delicious.

102, Street 2. Tel: (053) 952 862. Open: 6.30am–10pm.

La Villa ★★

Fine dining in a fine setting, La Villa offers breakfast, lunch and dinner, each with a selection of either European or Asian delights. Choose to sit in the leafy garden or indoors in a beautifully decorated colonial room. A reasonable wine list accompanies a wide selection of cocktails.

185 Pom Romchek 5 Kom. Tel: (053) 730 151.

Open: 7–9am, noon–2pm, 6.30–9pm.

ENTERTAINMENT
Riverside Balcony Bar
Lots of old wicker chairs and tables in an old wooden house overlooking the Sangker River, the Riverside Balcony is a great location to while away the evening hours. The food is a little limited, but the beer is ice cold and it's a good place to meet fellow travellers.
165, Street 1, south end of town. Tel: (053) 730 313. Open: 4–11pm.

GETTING AWAY FROM IT ALL
Kirirom
ACCOMMODATION
Kirirom Hillside Resort ★★★
If you intend visiting Kirirom National Park, one of Cambodia's best, then this is the place to stay. Located next to the park entrance, the resort offers a number of different accommodation options including bungalows, wooden cabins and luxury villas. It's also possible to camp in the grounds; the resort provides the tents and full use of all its facilities which include a swimming pool and spa.
Phum Thmey, Chambak, Phnom Srouch (24km (15 miles) west of National Route 4). Tel: (016) 59 999. Email: info@ kiriromresort.com. www.kiriromresort.com

Koh Kong
ACCOMMODATION
Asean Hotel ★★
A clean, comfortable hotel overlooking the river, the Asean's rooms all include air-conditioning, satellite TV and mini-bar.
2 Village, Smach Mean Chey. Tel: (035) 936 666. Email: aseanhotel@ netkhmer.com. http://aseanhotel. netkhmer.com
Oasis Resort ★★
Beautifully located near the river, this selection of bungalows to the north of the main town offers a pleasant getaway. All bungalows are air-conditioned and the resort has a great pool plus an adequate bar and restaurant. *1km (0.6 miles) north of the bridge and Sihanoukville boat pier. Tel: (016) 331 556. Email: oasisresort@ netkhmer.com. http://oasisresort. netkhmer.com*

Kratie
ACCOMMODATION
Santepheap Hotel ★
A comfortable option, the Santepheap is well located in the heart of Kratie town and tends to attract any tour groups passing through. Facilities are limited, but this is to be expected in this town just awakening to tourism.
Preah Sumamarit Road. Tel: (072) 971 537.

EATING OUT
Red Sun Falling ★
Backpacker heaven in Kratie, the food includes good Western breakfasts and a few local dishes. Desserts include great chocolate brownies and pineapple pie. The Red Sun doubles as a second-hand bookshop.
Preah Sumamarit Road. Open: 7.30am–2pm & 5–11pm.

Index

Acknowledgements

Thomas Cook Publishing wishes to thank CPA MEDIA/DAVID HENLEY for the photographs in this book, to whom the copyright belongs, except for the following images:

DREAMSTIME V Pomortzeff 1; J Van Ostaeyen 93; D. Kushch 130

For CAMBRIDGE PUBLISHING MANAGEMENT LTD:
Project editor: Diane Teillol
Typesetter: Trevor Double
Copy-editor: Debbie Stowe
Proofreader: Kelly Walker
Indexer: Marie Lorimer

SEND YOUR THOUGHTS TO
BOOKS@THOMASCOOK.COM

We're committed to providing the very best up-to-date information in our travel guides and constantly strive to make them as useful as they can be. You can help us to improve future editions by letting us have your feedback. If you've made a wonderful discovery on your travels that we don't already feature, if you'd like to inform us about recent changes to anything that we do include, or if you simply want to let us know your thoughts about this guidebook and how we can make it even better – we'd love to hear from you.

Send us ideas, discoveries and recommendations today and then look out for your valuable input in the next edition of this title.

Emails to the above address, or letters to Travellers Series Editor, Thomas Cook Publishing, PO Box 227, Unit 9, Coningsby Road, Peterborough PE3 8SB, UK.

Please don't forget to let us know which title your feedback refers to!